JACK STEIN'S

World on a Plate

for Lucy and Bocca

JACK STEIN'S

World on a Plate

with photography by
Paul Winch-Furness

introduction

The recipes that appear within this book are my own versions of ones that I have loved throughout my life and which I return to time and time again. Recipes that never fail me, bringing comfort and pleasure and sometimes simply reminding me of moments shared with friends and family.

For those who are anticipating purity or unadulterated authenticity then there is, I'm sorry to say, disappointment ahead – most of the recipes here have been finessed by me, sometimes fiddled around with and occasionally radically overhauled. But the reasons for so doing have always been driven by a passion to develop the perfect flavour combination and gastro-pleasure hit. Simple deliciousness in other words!

We all have an earliest food memory. Mine is oysters! I was three or four years old and on holiday with my family in France. My elder brother Ed was given a fresh oyster and swallowed it whole. So I had to have one – peer pressure works not only for games and dares but also for exploring the wonders of shellfish…

This book is in part a collection of culinary and gastronomic memories built around growing up in a prototypical foodie household with parents who spent three months of the year searching out new ideas and unexpected flavours for their restaurant back in Cornwall.

Unsurprisingly this experience had a profound effect on the way that I cook today. I quite simply see the world's food as a vast and wondrous palette with which to paint anything and everything I want.

As a child I loved observing my parents' passion for exploring the food markets of the world and the way that they delighted in experiencing new ingredients and exotic sauces and spices. Bit by bit the world they discovered began to come back into their restaurant kitchen and many of the classical rules went back out.

They, and we, became food travellers. Every December bags were packed, passports assembled and travel arrangements confirmed and off we set, Jules Verne like, around the world in 80 days. My parents, who for nine months of the year were so busy that they were virtual strangers to their three offspring, were for the next three months our constant companions and fellow adventurers. Our way was usually East to Australia via India, Thailand and Hong Kong, then on to the Americas and home. By which time, it has to be said, we were fairly sick of each other and eager to get back to the reassuring normality of our Cornish fishing village.

This intense food and travel experience, year after year, became part of who I am, and though the precise details of the trips escape me now the flavours and sensations have stayed with me ever since. Because of this, when I am playing around in the kitchen I find it very easy to switch between say Singapore, Mexico, Thailand or India. So I have no problem with using the influences and flavours I experienced on my travels when cooking European or British dishes at home. In fact I revel in it. My Sunday roast gravy, for example, includes soy sauce, Thai fish sauce, kecap manis sauce and star anise – and it's wonderful.

My parents repeatedly advised me not to become a chef. I think they feared that the long hours and harsh and sometimes brutal conditions weren't for me and that the fragile and delicate creature they had brought into the world deserved a life of study and contemplation. So after finishing school I set off to Cardiff University to read psychology. But during this time away in academia I discovered that I could not only cook but also had a passion to learn more about the physiology and psychology of taste and smell. It was the time of food academics like Harold McGee and chefs such as Heston Blumenthal and Ferran Adria.

I was hooked – at least in theory.

My initial foray into formal chef training spurred me into questioning accepted assumptions about food and flavour. Why always lemon with fish? Why always add salt to sauces to bring out flavour?

Once established with the basic techniques and rules of the professional kitchen I set off fairly sure that the Michelin Guide world and its stars was to be my destiny. I found my way into kitchens in Paris, Sydney and the south of France.

Thankfully and fortuitously it didn't take long for me to realise that I had picked the wrong guide and the wrong guiding star system to be led by, and that my parents had been right all along. Take amazing local ingredients, tell their story on a plate and don't mess around with them too much.

I hope that this book will show that it is perfectly possible, perhaps even desirable, to look back and celebrate our recent history in food and cooking whilst at the same time hoping to move the conversation on and hopefully up.

I was immensely proud of my dad's book *Rick Stein's Food Heroes* which came out in the early 2000s because it was a rallying cry to the British public to 'use or lose' bespoke and artisan. It has helped enable my generation of chefs to have the best raw ingredients with which to build our dishes. Its influence has also ensured that the general cooking public has the same building blocks as the professionals when it comes to creating wonderful dishes in the kitchen.

So hold on tight to the simple philosophy of taking the best possible ingredients, treating them with respect and having fun with them. And if you are the kind of cook who doesn't like being bound by the old ways and enjoys experimenting with new flavours and techniques from around the world then this book is most definitely for you.

Thirty years of being front and centre as my parents built one of the most successful restaurants in Britain gives me a great sense of pride in their achievement and in the legacy they have passed on to me and my two brothers Ed and Charlie as well as to the industry in which they work.

This book is a proud product of my culinary upbringing and comes with a pedigree which I hope shines through every page.

Enjoy!

Jack Stein
Cornwall, 2018

11

travel

Without travel this book would not exist, and I would
be a different and, to my mind, a less complete individual.
I believe very strongly that when you travel to a new
country it is through the food that you can most
profoundly link your experience with the culture and the
people that live there. So many times in my life I have sat
eating with the street hawkers or local tuk-tuk drivers
and have watched the cooks, and found myself able to
communicate through food alone. It is universal, and I
thank my parents for the amount of travel we did when
we were young. Admittedly it wasn't always easy. For
example, being 11 years old and seeing the poverty in India
for the first time was tough, but I think it's essential to face
such problems even if you are too young to comprehend
completely what is happening.

More and more people are travelling, as children,
as young adults or when retired, and so are experiencing
the variety of food on offer. I think this book will speak
to everyone who has travelled – even a little – because
you will understand so many of the flavours, even if you
have never before had, for example, a gado-gado made
with British winter vegetables! I think travel does broaden
the mind, but the combination of food and travel broadens
the mind and the palate!

A selection of my travel photos, including
my favourite feasts and delicious dishes.

sourcing

So to begin, let's talk about sourcing.

Part of the revolution in British food has been the quality of all the ingredients available, not only to chefs but also to home cooks. I believe that the key to any dish you cook is the raw ingredients, and this is where you should start. Take your time and find the best butcher, fishmonger or fruit and veg shop. Talk to your suppliers, even if it's in a supermarket; go to the butcher's counter, rather than taking the pre-packed meat. Trust me when I say this is the biggest commitment that I ask of you from this book; I've done my best to make the recipes as easy and fun to make as possible, so if you make the effort to source top-quality ingredients, the results should be delicious.

I was sitting on Canggu Beach, in Bali, a few years ago eating a chicken satay; the sun was going down and I remember thinking this was the best satay I had ever eaten. But then I thought, 'Is it really?' The whole scene was amazing, but the chicken itself wasn't anything like a great herb-fed British chicken thigh, and it was tough and lacking in flavour. This was the moment when I realised this book needed to be written. I am not the only one using this eclectic approach; most of the best restaurants in the country do this and have done so for ages: Michelin-starred restaurants look to the Far East for flavourings; trendy new restaurants use American BBQ techniques with rare-breed animals; and plant-based restaurants use flavour and techniques from all food cultures to create outstanding dishes.

I get a lot of pleasure from selecting first-class ingredients (it's the main part of my job, to be honest), and I think you will too. The great produce we get in the UK can be used in so many exciting, innovative ways. Amazing rare- breed pork can be turned into incredible Thai food; our wonderful white fish goes perfectly in a Baja fish taco; and winter vegetables are perfect for an Indonesian gado-gado – there is much to explore!

sustainability

In selecting ingredients, we must always be guided by considerations of sustainability. Whatever we choose, whether animal or vegetable, should be in season and plentiful, so that we do not endanger a species or the ecosystem by using it. The first (and I still think best) lesson I heard about sustainability came from Raymond Blanc talking in the early days of the Sustainable Restaurant Association (SRA), founded in 2010. He said that we cannot all be experts in sustainability; it is a learning process. We need to trust our suppliers, but we should also visit them, audit them and make sure they are who they say they are. Times change, and the conversation evolves. I clearly remember that back in the 1980s and 1990s shark was on the menu at The Seafood Restaurant. Today it seems completely crazy that we were eating sharks – which include many endangered species – but such changes in people's attitudes can't be achieved overnight, by dogmatic methods. What Raymond was saying is that we keep learning; and the SRA, with its 'Food Made Good' initiative, is a great guide that we can learn from and journey with on the route to sustainability.

When it comes to sustainability, there are some simple, common-sense rules to follow. First, seek advice from such ecologically focused groups as the Marine Stewardship Council (MSC), Red Tractor, Fairtrade and the Rainforest Alliance. But keep monitoring their advice, as situations do change. For example, North Sea cod recently became MSC certified (so out of danger), whereas wild sea bass became a species to avoid.

Secondly, when it comes to animals, be aware of the breeding and rearing conditions of species you want to cook with. Some species, especially certain kinds of fish, may be better left off the menu at certain times of the year. Choose to eat less meat, but of high quality, such as free-range chickens and grass-fed beef, rather than larger quantities of cheaper meat produced in poor conditions.

Thirdly, get to know the story of the produce. Visit the butcher, the farmer and the fish market. You want to tell their story on your plate. Understand why you should use all the cuts of the fish, animal or plant. A butcher cannot just give you ribeye steaks all the time; take the cheek and the brisket and the rump when you can. Learn about the various cuts and how best to maximise their flavour through different techniques. This book may seem a little meat-heavy, but I have chosen to use as many different cuts as possible.

Fourth, buy locally; but give your business to good, ethically-run companies that source from your area. There will always be times when that business has to get things that are out of season or not local, but the money it earns stays within your community, so the retailer can give more business during the high season to small growers and producers.

Fifth, challenge yourself to produce vegetarian, even vegan, dishes. This book doesn't contain many of these, but I have made an effort to understand these types of food and try to eat more of them. I recommend that you do also.

Lastly, try to learn as much as possible about agriculture, aquaculture and wild food. Choose game when in season; choose farmed fish where the inputs are good quality and based on ecological systems such as we are seeing in Europe.

a note on measurements and seasoning

In this book we employ a few different measurements, but I have to say I much prefer to use grams for everything. In order to follow a recipe all you need is a set of scales. As a general rule, a litre of water weighs a kilo, a tablespoon is 15g, but it's more accurate to weigh liquids, so buy some scales and throw away the measuring jugs and cups.

When it comes to salt, I recommend following a simple rule of using 1 per cent of salt in proportion to the rest of the ingredients. For example, if everything weighs 1kg, you need 10g of salt.

When I'm cooking, I add salt little and often. Every time a new ingredient goes into the bowl or pan, season it a little. If you wait and season at the end of cooking, you'll miss the depth of flavour required. Also, when you have finished cooking, season the main ingredient again with a little salt; I like to call it finishing salt, and always use it in my dishes.

essentials in my kitchen

Sourcing the best ingredients is the first step to creating a superb dish. You must also have good-quality equipment for preparing them.

a probe This is basically a digital thermometer that tells you the internal temperature of whatever it is that you are cooking. For example, if you want medium-rare beef, it should read 56°C in the centre of the meat. For fish on the bone I cook to 55°C. I implore you to buy one of these; they are cheap and will make this book one hell of a lot easier to understand and follow. I always cook to a temperature, not a time.

knives 'You never cut yourself on a sharp knife,' I was told. Well it turns out that you can, but you're more likely to if the knife isn't sharp enough for the job! Buy good ones. I use great Japanese-style knives made by I. O. Shen. Buy a sharpener or a Fischer sharpening block if several people in the house are going to use your knives. If only you will be using it, get a steel and sharpen with that – and don't let other people sharpen your knifes.

mandoline This very sharp cutting tool slices ingredients really finely. They are relatively inexpensive, and some come with add-ons for making courgette spaghetti or whatever is currently trendy in the foodie world.

pans Buy the best you can afford; the thicker the metal, the less likely they are to burn when you are reducing a sauce.

blowtorch I recommend getting a MAPP gas gun from a builders' warehouse. They burn at a higher temperature than butane and do not taint the food. Well worth the investment.

scales A good set of digital scales makes all cooking more simple and ensures consistent results.

my playlist essentials

I always listen to music while I cook and here are some of my favourites that made it on to my playlist while I was writing the book!

1   Always the Sun – The Stranglers
2   Night Moves – Bob Seger
3   Fluorescent Adolescent – Arctic Monkeys
4   Brick House – Commodores
5   On – Aphex Twin
6   Getting Away With It – Electronic
7   One – Metallica
8   The Body of an American – The Pogues
9   It's the End of the World – REM
10 Keeping Warm – We Were Promised Jetpacks
11 Lithium – Nirvana
12 Boys of Summer – Don Henley
13 Nothing but Flowers – Talking Heads
14 Change – Blind Melon
15 Sir Duke – Stevie Wonder
16 Soul to Squeeze – Red Hot Chilli Peppers
17 Original Nuttah – Shy FX
18 Linoleum – NOFX
19 Something – Beatles
20 Always on my Mind – Elvis Presley

street food, tapas & snacks

veggie crisps with beetroot hummus

These tasty little snacks are well worth the little effort it takes to make them. They will keep for up to a month if sealed in a dry, airtight jar, and they can be used to add crunch to anything.

You really need a mandoline for this recipe to ensure you get the veggies thin enough to crisp. You could use a very sharp knife, but you might not get the same result.

SERVES 8

2 sweet potatoes
2 tablespoons olive oil
2 beetroots
a bunch of kale (about 250g)
2 tablespoons grated
    Parmesan
sea salt

for the beetroot hummus
1 (400g) can chickpeas,
    drained
1 tablespoon tahini paste
juice of ½ lemon
2 garlic cloves, peeled and
    roughly chopped
3 tablespoons olive oil
3 large cooked beetroots
salt and pepper

Preheat the oven to 180°C Fan (200°C/Gas Mark 6).

Peel the sweet potato and slice thinly using a mandoline. Place the slices between kitchen paper to soak up any excess moisture then place in a bowl, tossing to coat with ½ tablespoon oil. Season with a pinch of sea salt and then lay the slices out on a non-stick baking tray.

Repeat the process for the beetroot, and use a second baking tray if there is not room on the first.

Place the sweet potato and beetroot slices in the oven for 10 minutes, and then swap the two trays over to make sure one isn't browning more than the other. Bake for another 5–10 minutes. Once they are golden brown, remove from the oven and allow to sit for a few minutes; they will crisp up more as they cool.

Tear the kale leaves into medium-sized pieces, similar in size to the crisps. In a bowl mix together the Parmesan and remaining oil and add the kale, stirring to coat the leaves. Spread the kale out in a single layer on a baking tray and bake in the oven for about 10 minutes until crispy. Remove the kale crisps from the oven and allow to cool. Season with a pinch of sea salt if needed (the Parmesan might make them salty enough).

Meanwhile make the beetroot hummus. Put the chickpeas, tahini paste, lemon juice, garlic, olive oil, beetroots, salt and pepper into a food processor. Blend together until smooth, adding more oil if needed. Taste and add more salt/lemon/oil if necessary.

Serve the crisps with the beetroot hummus.

gado gado with british winter vegetables

An Indonesian classic which is very simple to prepare and is quite similar to a vegetarian satay. This version is something I created as a way of using and celebrating our great winter vegetables whilst combining them with the culinary magic of gado gado. Vegetables such as Brussels sprouts and kale, which have a wonderful flavour when just partially or barely cooked, work really well. If you find colourful and different kales and brassicas, you can make a vibrantly inviting dish to put on the table as the nights begin to close in.

This is also a super-healthy dish and can be made vegan by simply removing the eggs.

SERVES 4

for the peanut sauce dressing
150g unsalted roasted
   peanuts
2 tablespoons vegetable oil
2 shallots, finely chopped
2 garlic cloves, crushed
2 teaspoons finely grated
   palm sugar
1 teaspoon tamarind paste
1 tablespoon lime juice
1 tablespoon fish sauce
1 teaspoon shrimp paste
1 (270ml) can of
   coconut milk
salt and pepper

for the winter vegetables
150g January King cabbage
   or similar
150g purple-sprouting or
   tenderstem broccoli
1 tablespoon vegetable oil
100g Brussel sprouts, halved
200g cooked baby potatoes,
   quartered

to garnish
4 eggs
a handful of coriander,
   chopped (optional)

Place the peanuts in a blender or food processor and blitz to a fine crumb. Heat the oil in a frying pan and soften the shallots and garlic in it. Add the peanuts and all the remaining sauce ingredients and bring together. Check the seasoning.

Semi-hard-boil the eggs: place them in boiling water for 6 minutes, then refresh in iced water and peel them. Cut them in half.

Cook the cabbage and broccoli separately in salted water until they are just softened but still crisp (no more than 2 minutes). Refresh in iced water. Meanwhile, heat the oil in a frying pan over a medium-high heat and add the sprouts, frying until lightly browned. Once golden brown, remove and place on kitchen paper to remove any excess oil.

Toss all the vegetables together, place on a plate and top with the eggs. Dress with the peanut sauce and garnish with coriander, if using.

Cornish purple flowering sprouts. These would be delicious in the gado gado (see page 25).

huevos rancheros

I loved the food and culture of Mexico, and this classic Mexican breakfast dish is a must for all lovers of spice in the morning. When used to partner the best-quality free-range eggs, the spicy tomato sauce and tortilla with pickled jalapeños will wake you up with a chilli jolt and set you fair for the day ahead. Just remember that the sauce, though like ordinary and innocent tomato sauce in appearance, should be handled with caution.

SERVES 4

8 free-range eggs
1 tablespoon sunflower oil,
     plus more if needed
a knob of butter
8 (10cm) corn or
     flour tortillas
salt and pepper

for the tomato sauce

2 garlic cloves, finely
     chopped
1 red chilli, finely chopped
1 onion, finely chopped
1 tablespoon sunflower oil
1 teaspoon salt
1 (400g) can of chopped
     tomatoes
1 teaspoon Marmite
a pinch of five-spice powder

to garnish

1 avocado, peeled, stone
     removed and sliced
a little chopped fresh
     coriander
120ml soured cream
pickled jalapeños, to taste

First make the tomato sauce. Sauté the garlic, chilli and onion in the oil in a frying pan, adding the salt, until soft but not coloured. Then add the tomatoes, Marmite and five-spice and simmer until reduced and thick.

Sauté the eggs in the oil and season. When they are nearly cooked, add the butter to the pan and spoon the melted butter over them. You might need to do this in batches, depending on the size of your pan.

Meanwhile, heat a frying pan over a medium heat and warm the tortillas for 10–20 seconds each. Keep warm as you heat each one before you serve.

Spread the tomato sauce over the tortillas and top with an egg. Garnish with avocado, coriander, soured cream and jalapeños.

clam po' boys

Po' boys are a fast food dish from the Deep South of the United States. A part of the world that does fast food, and especially Po' boys, really well. My father, after filming his *Seafood Odyssey*, brought back a recipe for Po' boys with great excitement. It was the first time I'd encountered a deep-fried seafood sandwich, and I was smitten. This recipe works very well with our British clams though mussels, oysters or prawns would work just as well. The key is to *panne* them properly, with Japanese panko breadcrumbs.

A perfect dish for a sunny summer afternoon helped along with a glass of good beer.

MAKES 4

2 baguettes cut in half, or 4
   individual baguettes
1kg clams
25g seasoned flour
2 eggs, beaten
150g panko breadcrumbs
vegetable oil for deep frying
150g miso mayonnaise (see
   page 252)
½ medium-sized lettuce,
   finely sliced
1 red onion, pickled
   (see Jack's house pickle,
   page 257)
salt and pepper

Slice each baguette lengthways and toast the slices face down in a griddle pan. Steam open the clams in a little water till just open. Remove the clams from their shells and pat dry. Place the flour, beaten egg and breadcrumbs on separate plates; dredge the clams in flour, then the egg and finally the breadcrumbs.

Heat the oil to 180°C. Drop the clams into the oil and fry until golden brown in small batches. Transfer to kitchen paper and season with sea salt.

Spread the mayonnaise on the baguette slices and top with lettuce and then the crispy clams. Scatter with the pickled onions and enjoy!

deep-fried helford river prawns with aioli

Every September in Cornwall we finally get one of the year's most eagerly awaited migrations. Thousands of tiny prawns start arriving in the Helford River and, once caught, come to our restaurant en masse. They are the sweetest little prawns you will ever taste.

   The best way to serve prawns, including these little Cornish gems, is simply with some smoked paprika and freshly made garlicky aioli. We deep-fry them and eat everything, including the head and the shell. The best flavour is to be found in the shell and is delicious, so don't let it go to waste.

SERVES 4

vegetable or sunflower oil, for
   deep frying
600g river prawns or small
   tiger prawns
1 teaspoon smoked paprika
sea salt

for the aioli

100g miso mayonnaise (see
   page 252)
2 garlic cloves, finely minced
a pinch of smoked paprika

to garnish

2 lemons, cut into wedges
1 tablespoon chopped flat-
   leaf parsley (optional)

First make the aioli. Put the miso mayo in a large ramekin and stir through the garlic. Sprinkle over the paprika and keep in the fridge until ready to serve.

Heat the oil in a deep fryer or a saucepan to 180°C. Pat the prawns dry using kitchen paper, then deep-fry the prawns for 2 minutes. Remove from the oil and transfer to kitchen paper to drain any excess. Once drained, season with salt and paprika.

Serve the prawns with the aioli and lemon wedges alongside, with parsley scattered over the top.

cornish lobster roll

This is one of the dishes in the book that showcases my passion for using great British produce with a 'world' twist. Our lobsters from Cornwall are the best – in America these rolls are served with Canadian lobsters but make no mistake the North Atlantic lobster is a far finer creature.

I find this to be a great dish for a picnic – it can be served cold, and is ideal for making one or two lobsters go a very long way. The miso mayonnaise is wonderfully savoury, though you will need to add a good amount of acidity to cut through the richness.

So load up the rolls and watch as your guests hungrily feed their faces with lashings of lobster and mayo!

SERVES 4

2 (600g) lobsters, live
50g butter, melted
juice of 1 lemon
a pinch of five-spice powder
4 (hot dog style) brioche rolls
1 tablespoon chopped chives
1 tablespoon chopped
   tarragon
4 tablespoons miso
   mayonnaise (see page 252)
salt

to serve
chips
green salad
mayo

Chill the lobsters in the fridge for a few hours, in their original packaging. Bring a big pan of salted water (50g salt per litre) to the boil. Plunge the lobsters into the boiling water, covered, and cook for 8 minutes. Transfer them to a chopping board and allow to cool.

Using a heavy knife, remove the head and claws, and break the tail in half by pushing it together lengthways. This will split it along the back. Peel away the shell and remove the dark intestinal thread running down the tail. Crack the claws with the back of a heavy knife and pick out the meat using a lobster pick. Each lobster should yield about 300g meat.

In a bowl mix the butter, lemon juice, five-spice powder and 1 teaspoon salt. Add the lobster meat and stir it through so it is well coated.

Toast the buns and cut a little extra out of the middle to accommodate the filling. Mix the herbs and miso mayonnaise with the marinated lobster meat and fill the rolls with this. Serve the rolls with chips and salad and extra mayo on the side.

cornish chilli crab

Singapore, in many ways, is where it all really began for me. Our family had travelled in Europe and eaten oysters and other *fruits de mer* in Brittany and beyond but in 1985, on a trip to Australia when I was five, my love of seafood really took off. On a stopover in Singapore we went, as usual, to a night market and that's where I first saw and tasted chilli crab. Maybe it was the jet lag, maybe the unbelievable humidity, but something in the experience opened my senses. I knew crabs, but not like these. Those watching me in the market might have been confused to see a small, pale, ginger-haired kid looking perplexed by his sensory overload, but in fact I was being seduced by the wonderful flavours that the crab dish had to offer. Ever since I have found the combination of eating Asian food at 11pm while jet-lagged to be paradise – and I owe it all to this dish!

My father's version of chilli crab uses brown crab, which is far fuller-flavoured than the mud crabs used in Singapore. My own recipe is similar to his but with a few tweaks – a classic but with just a little twist.

SERVES 4

2kg boiled brown crab
4 tablespoons groundnut or
  sunflower oil
4 garlic cloves, finely
  chopped
2.5cm fresh root ginger,
  finely chopped
3 medium-hot, red, Dutch
  chillies, finely chopped
4 tablespoons tomato
  ketchup
2 tablespoons dark soy sauce
1 teaspoon Marmite
2 spring onions, cut into
  5cm pieces and finely
  shredded lengthways
a handful of chopped
  coriander

Put the crab on its back on the chopping board, so that the claws and softer body section face upwards, then simply twist off the main claws, leaving the legs attached to the body. Now put your thumbs against the hard shell, close to the crab's tail, and push and prise the body section out and away from the shell. The legs should still be attached to the body. Remove the small stomach sac situated just behind the crab's mouth and pull away the feather-like gills ('dead man's fingers') which are attached along the edges of the centre part; discard these.

Using a teaspoon, scoop out the brown meat from inside the shell; reserve.

Chop the body into quarters and then cut the main claws in half at the joint. Crack the shells of each piece with a hammer or the blunt edge of a large knife.

Heat the oil, garlic, ginger and chilli in a wok for 1 minute to release their aromas.

Next, turn up the heat and fry off the brown crab meat, then add the ketchup, soy sauce, Marmite and 150ml water. These all add savoury and sweet notes to the finished dish. Now add the remaining crab in its shell and stir-fry the crab for 2 minutes. Remove from the heat and finish with spring onions and chopped coriander.

Serve immediately – with lots of finger bowls and napkins, as this is a messy dish.

hong kong stir-fried crab with garlic and chilli

This is one of those dishes that you just have to have when you're in Hong Kong. When I'm there, I am usually either hung-over or jet-lagged – or most likely a combination of the two – and that means I just have to seek out these crabs as they seem to be the only thing to help me with both of my temporary afflictions.

There is an amazing amount of garlic on these crabs and they can be blisteringly hot! I've found the only way to temper the heat is with the classic Chinese hangover beer Tsing Tao.

I have substituted our local brown crabs for the Asian crabs. They have much more meat in the claws and the flavour is far superior. Interestingly, the last time I was in Hong Kong I saw some of our British brown crabs being sold in a local market – clearly their fame has spread to such an extent that even the Chinese are starting to demand them!

SERVES 4

4 cooked crabs, each about
    900g, jointed into pieces
50g dried black beans
    (prepared and cooked
    according to packet
    instructions)
50ml soy sauce
150ml rice wine or dry sherry
5 spring onions, sliced

to serve
20 garlic cloves, minced
100ml sunflower oil
5 whole dry Kashmiri chillies
rice (optional)

Fry the minced garlic in the oil until golden (avoid frying it longer, which would make it bitter). Strain through a sieve and dry the garlic on kitchen paper.

Slice the chillies and fry in the same oil until crisp. Remove from the pan and drain on kitchen paper.

Pour about 200ml water into a wok, add the crab pieces, cover and steam over a high heat until they are warm (do this in batches if necessary), then add the black beans, soy sauce and rice wine or sherry. Cook through for 5 minutes, then add the spring onions.

Garnish the crabs with the chilli and garlic over (and in) the crab shells, and serve with rice on the side.

crab omelette

I was once about to do a demo at the Padstow Christmas Festival and after a long hard day found myself slightly under the influence of some local cider and unsure what to cook for the assembled crowd. A great chef and friend, Carl Clarke, just kept whispering 'crab omelette' in my ear. I vaguely remembered having had one in Sri Lanka but had no recipe to hand – so I made it up on the spot. It proved a great success and here it is in all it's inspired glory!

SERVES 1

3 eggs
20ml double cream
1 teaspoon soy sauce
25g butter
50g white crab
10g brown crab
a few fresh curry leaves
a handful of chopped
  fresh coriander
salt

Whisk the eggs in a bowl, then stir in the cream and soy sauce. Heat the butter in a frying pan until foaming, then add the egg mixture, tilting the pan slightly from side to side so the egg mix covers the bottom. When the egg mix is half cooked and almost set, add the crab and the herbs. Using a spatula fold the omelette in half and leave for 30 seconds then slide onto a plate to serve. (The residual heat will finish cooking the inside of the omelette.) Finish with a little salt and then enjoy.

monkfish rice and curry

I have been to Sri Lanka many times and I absolutely love the place. The food is wonderful, the people are amazing and the surf is great. In the English winter it's my go-to spot if I am in need of some sun.

Everywhere there are signs offering 'rice and curry' – often more rice than curry. Add one or two of the wonderful sambals and a few chutneys on offer and a frugal and brilliant meal is to be had.

I use monkfish in this recipe which is meatier and less susceptible to overcooking than many other fish. I find it to be the perfect partner in a fish curry as it is quite bland and so handles the spice extremely well. Try to find fresh curry leaves as they really do give the taste of Sri Lanka. Serve with bowls of plain rice and poppadoms.

SERVES 4

50ml vegetable oil
4 onions
12 curry leaves
6 garlic cloves, finely
   chopped
5cm ginger, finely chopped
8 vine-ripened tomatoes,
   sliced
400ml coconut milk
600g monkfish cut into
   4 fillets, trimmed
1 tablespoon salt
2 green chillies, sliced

for the Sri Lankan curry powder

2 tablespoons basmati rice
4 tablespoons coriander
   seeds
3 tablespoons cumin seeds
2 tablespoons black
   peppercorns
2 tablespoons chilli flakes
1 teaspoon fenugreek seeds
1 tablespoon black
   mustard seeds
2 teaspoons cloves
1 heaped teaspoon
   cardamom seeds (from
   the pods)
1 heaped teaspoon
   fennel seeds
1 teaspoon turmeric

to serve

boiled basmati rice
deep-fried poppadom
   triangles

To make the curry powder, place the rice in a dry pan and roast until brown. Then add the spices and cook together until fragrant. Place in a blender and mix. Store in an airtight container until needed; it will keep for 1 month.

For the curry base, warm half of the vegetable oil in a large, wide pan and add the onions and 6 of the curry leaves; cook until lightly coloured (8 minutes). Then add the garlic and ginger and cook for another 3 minutes. Move this onion mixture to one side of the pan and place 2–3 teaspoons of the roasted curry powder (depending how hot you like it) in the space left. Cook the spices for 1 minute (this deepens their flavour), then add the tomatoes and stir together.

Cook the mixture for a further 20 minutes. (Meanwhile boil the rice, then cover to keep warm.)

If the curry starts to dry, add a little water. You want the tomatoes to break down and release their juice. Now add the coconut milk and cook until reduced and thick. Keep the curry warm over a low heat while you cook the fish.

Season the monkfish fillets with the salt and cook in a frying pan in the remaining vegetable oil until nicely browned; you want to cook it under the temperature where you want it to finish – say 45°C. Take the fillets out of the pan, slice thickly and leave to rest.

Warm up the curry base and add the monkfish slices to the pan. Cook for 1–2 minutes until the fish reaches 55°C. Remove from the heat. Add the raw sliced chilli and remaining fresh curry leaves. Serve with the basmati rice and deep-fried poppadom triangles.

fish finger sandwich

A simple snack, but one of my favourites as it reminds me of being a child. If I'm honest, I do like the ones made by a famous bearded sailor too, but making your own is great fun and kids love them.

SERVES 4

25g seasoned flour
1 egg, beaten
75g panko breadcrumbs
400g cod fillet, skin removed,
  cut into goujons 10 x 5cm
sunflower oil for frying
8 slices of white bread
4 tablespoons tartare sauce
  (see page 152)
4 tablespoons ketchup
1 Baby Gem lettuce,
  shredded
sea salt

to serve
chips

Put the flour, egg and breadcrumbs in separate shallow bowls. Coat the goujons in the flour, shake off any excess and then dip them into the egg, to coat all over. Finally coat them in the breadcrumbs.

Heat the oil in a frying pan (you need enough oil to come about 2cm up the side of your pan), and when hot (when a breadcrumb sizzles if dropped in), fry the goujons. Do this in batches if necessary.

Spread tartare sauce on one piece of bread and ketchup on the other. Place the fish on the tartare sauce, season with sea salt and place the lettuce on top. Add the other slice of bread and cut the sandwich in half diagonally.

Serve with chips (of course!)

cornish cod tacos with soured clotted cream

Dad promised us much when we were growing up, but one thing he promised that never materialised was a trip to Mexico's Baja Peninsula. He did come up with a recipe for Baja Fish Tacos though – not quite the same as going there but they are still one of my favourite things to eat.

I've made this version using our line-caught cod from Newlyn; it is similar to the mahi-mahi that they use in Mexico but, in my opinion, superior.

Continuing in the spirit of finding great British alternatives to world ingredients, here I use some soured Cornish clotted cream thinned with a little milk – feel free to substitute standard soured cream.

MAKES 8

400g cod fillets
sunflower oil, for pan- and
    deep-frying
8 soft flour tortillas
sea salt and freshly ground
    black pepper

for the pico de gallo

1 red onion, finely chopped
5 tomatoes, skinned,
    deseeded and finely
    chopped
3 or 4 medium-hot red
    chillies, deseeded and
    finely chopped
1 teaspoon caster sugar
juice of 1 lime
4 tablespoons chopped
    coriander
a pinch of salt

for the batter

225g plain flour
2 eggs
a pinch of salt

for the pickled lettuce

350ml cider vinegar
1 teaspoon sugar
1 teaspoon salt
a pinch of thyme
a pinch of chilli flakes
3 juniper berries
225g iceberg lettuce,
    finely shredded

for the soured clotted cream

100ml clotted cream
50ml full-fat milk
juice of 1 lime

First make the pico de gallo (salsa) by mixing together all the ingredients in a bowl. Set aside.

Cut the fish fillets across into strips 1cm wide; season with plenty of salt and pepper.

For the batter, put the flour, eggs, salt and 200ml water into a bowl and mix until smooth.

For the pickled lettuce, mix all of the ingredients except the lettuce in a saucepan with 120ml water. Add the shredded lettuce to the liquid, bring to the boil, then remove from the heat and allow to cool.

To make the soured clotted cream, mix the clotted cream and milk together and stir in the lime juice.

Pour the sunflower oil into a frying pan (you need enough to be about 2cm deep), and heat over a medium heat. Fry the fish fillets for approximately 1 minute on each side. Drain on kitchen paper.

Warm the tortillas in a low oven or a microwave.

Heat the oil for deep-frying to around 180°C (355°F). Dip the strips of fish into the batter and then drop them into the hot oil and fry for 4 minutes, until crisp and golden. Lift out with a slotted spoon and drain briefly on kitchen paper.

To serve, put some pickled lettuce down the centre of each tortilla, top with the fried fish, then spoon over some pico de gallo and soured cream. Fold over two opposite sides of the tortilla, then fold over the other sides as tightly as possible. Serve straight away.

indonesian hot chicken soup soyo ayam

When I'm in Indonesia I often find myself getting a little bored with nasi goreng, delicious though it is. This chicken soup is the perfect alternative. It is well worth making your own basa gede, the Balinese spice paste – you can buy it quite easily, but it's just not the same.

For this recipe, the chicken you use needs to be free-range and of the very best quality you can afford. I like to play around with a soup for winter in England, using root vegetables; but for the summer, using a light vegetable such as spring onions is a great option.

SERVES 4

1 (1.4kg) chicken, quartered
2 lemongrass stalks, bashed
6 kaffir lime leaves
6 cloves garlic
1 tablespoon salt
2 tablespoons basa gede (see page 252), plus more if you like a chilli kick!
4 eggs
400g dried vermicelli noodles
100g bean sprouts
a handful of fresh coriander, leaves picked
a handful of Thai basil

to garnish
crispy shallots (see page 253)
1 chilli (optional), sliced into rings

Place the chicken, lemongrass, kaffir lime leaves, garlic, salt and 2 litres water in a large pot. Bring to the boil then reduce the heat and leave on a low simmer for 30 minutes, or until the a meat thermometer shows 70°C when inserted into the thickest part of the chicken. Remove the chicken and allow to cool. Strain the stock liquid into a jug, reserving the pot.

Once the chicken is cool enough to handle, pull the meat from the carcass into long shreds.

Fry the basa gede in the pot used for the chicken until fragrant (about 2 minutes). Remove from the heat and set aside.

Place the eggs in a clean pot and just cover with cold water; bring to the boil, then turn off the heat and leave the eggs in the water for another 4 minutes to cook in the residual heat. Remove the eggs, run them under cold water (this makes them easy to peel), then peel and set aside.

Now add the strained liquid from the chicken to the basa gede and heat to the boiling point (5 minutes). Meanwhile, cook the noodles according to the packet instructions.

Have ready 4 soup bowls. Just before serving, slice the eggs in half lengthways. Place some noodles in each bowl, top with the shredded chicken, and ladle over the stock. Add the bean sprouts, coriander leaves, basil and 2 egg halves. Garnish with the crispy shallots and a few slices of chilli, if using.

chicken thigh tacos and crispy skins

I use chicken thighs in this classic Mexican dish for their unbeatable flavour. They are married with some lovely five-spice-pickled red onions to give a beautiful colour. I much prefer to use the gluten free corn tortillas rather than ones made from flour.

Crispy chicken skin is very fashionable at the moment, which to me seems a bit bizarre because actually it doesn't taste quite as good as chicken skin that has been roasted on the bird and so is crispy in its natural way. However, if you remove the skin from the bird and oven-bake it you do get a lovely texture.

You can easily make these tacos with vegetables, such as courgettes perhaps or deep-fried carrots.

SERVES 4

8 chicken thighs (skin on, bone in)
2 teaspoons salt, plus extra as necessary
3 sprigs of thyme
2 tablespoons vegetable oil
12 (10cm-diameter) corn tortillas

to serve

4 tablespoons soured cream
5 tablespoons pico de gallo (see page 49)
1 avocado, sliced
1 red onion, pickled (see Jack's house pickle, page 257)
a handful of fresh coriander, roughly chopped (optional)
lime wedges

Prepare the chicken skin and thighs. Preheat the oven to 180°C Fan (200°C/Gas Mark 6).

Carefully remove the chicken skin from the thighs. Scrape off the chicken fat on the inside of the skins, being careful not to tear the skin. Now place the skins in a pot with 500ml cold water and add 1 teaspoon of salt and the thyme. Bring the water to the boil, then reduce the heat and leave to simmer for 30 minutes.

Remove the skin from the pan and pat dry to remove excess water. Lay the pieces skin side down on a baking tray and place a smaller baking tray on top. Place a couple of weights, such as cans of food, on top of this to flatten the chicken skin. Refrigerate for 1 hour.

Remove the tray from the fridge and take off the weights. Place the tray (still covered with the smaller baking tray) in the oven and bake for 25 minutes. Remove the smaller baking tray and turn over the skins. Put them back in the oven, uncovered, for another 20 minutes until golden.

Place the chicken thighs in a roasting tin and toss with half of the vegetable oil and the remaining teaspoon of salt; place it in the oven for 20 minutes. (This can be done at the same time as the second baking of the chicken skins.) Remove the chicken and skins from the oven. Place the skins on some kitchen paper to cool. Once the thighs are cool enough to handle, shred the meat, pulling it off the bone. Break the skin into pieces for topping the tacos.

Heat a frying pan on a high heat with the remaining oil and add the shredded chicken. Fry until golden brown and crispy (about 5 minutes). Season with salt.

Heat up the tortillas in the oven, at the previously set temperature, and place on the serving plates. Pile on the shredded chicken, soured cream, pico de gallo, avocado, crispy skin pieces, pickled onion and coriander. Squeeze over a little lime juice then wrap the tortilla around the fillings and tuck in!

pad thai

Pad thai is one of Thailand's national dishes and can be found all over Southeast Asia. This recipe is based on one from the city of Chiang Mai. I remember first having pad thai when I was about six years old in Bangkok, walking through the street food stalls around Sukhumvit. To my young palate it was amazing to taste the balance of sweetness from the chilli sauce and the acidity from the lime juice and tamarind; it's one of the first flavour sensations that I can remember. To some, being shepherded around the street markets of Bangkok at such a young age may seem like an idyllic childhood experience, but in reality it was often very tiring, and pad thai was the only food that kept me going.

I use chicken thighs for this recipe, as they have far more flavour than the breast meat.

SERVES 4

200g pad thai rice noodles
3 tablespoons vegetable oil
8 chicken thighs
3 tablespoons fish sauce
1 tablespoon palm sugar
1 tablespoon tamarind paste
juice of 2 limes
1 bird's-eye chilli,
    thinly sliced
3 garlic cloves, thinly sliced
5cm ginger root, sliced
2 eggs, beaten
2 tablespoons sweet
    chilli sauce

to garnish
6 spring onions
a handful of chopped roasted
    peanuts
crispy shallots (see page 253)
a handful of chopped fresh
    coriander
lime wedges

Soak the noodles in cold water for 1 hour. Drain and set aside.

Meanwhile, preheat the oven to 200°C Fan (220°C/Gas Mark 7).

Add 2 tablespoons vegetable oil to a roasting tin, then add the chicken thighs in a single layer. Cook them for 25 minutes until golden brown. Remove and allow to cool, then pull the meat off the bones in bite-sized pieces. Set aside.

In a saucepan combine the fish sauce, sugar, tamarind paste and lime juice and warm over a gentle heat to dissolve, forming a stock for the noodles.

Heat the remaining tablespoon of oil in a wok and stir-fry the chicken for 1 minute, then add the chilli, garlic and sliced ginger and fry for another 30 seconds.

Stir in the beaten eggs and allow to scramble, then add the noodles and stock and cook for 2 minutes until the noodles are soft (about 2 minutes).

Add the sweet chilli sauce and cook for another 1 minute. Garnish with spring onions, peanuts, shallots and coriander. Serve immediately with lime wedges on the side.

chicken wings with alabama white sauce

A few years ago my brother Charlie and I went on an eating and fact-finding trip to New York.

One day we walked down to the 9/11 Memorial and when we got there we found the sky very grey, adding an even greater sense of melancholy to the whole awful sadness of the experience. We had reservations at the Blue Smoke restaurant in Downtown as we wanted to sample their legendary chicken wings. We went in, having hardly spoken to each other for the best part of an hour, and ordered some beers and some wings. It was there that we had what we both consider one of the most sublime gastronomic experiences of our lives; the restorative effect of the chicken wings on two saddened individuals was epic. This is my homage to that NYC plate of wings.

Chicken wings are very cheap, and this dish is perfect for a barbecue or party. The miso is key because it gives a lovely round flavour to the otherwise quite acidic Alabama sauce. If you have the wherewithal, try smoking the wings – it makes them even better.

SERVES 4

16 chicken wings
2 tablespoons sunflower oil
2 teaspoons smoked paprika
2 teaspoons salt
2 teaspoons sugar

for the Alabama white sauce
200g mayonnaise
100ml cider vinegar
1 teaspoon salt
1 teaspoon sugar
$\frac{1}{2}$ teaspoon cayenne pepper
1 teaspoon fish sauce
1 teaspoon red miso paste

to serve
1 raw carrot, cut into batons

Preheat the oven to 220°C Fan (240°C/Gas Mark 9).

Place the wings on a baking tray and sprinkle the sunflower oil, paprika, salt and sugar on top. Mix everything well so all the wings are covered. Place the tray in the oven for 20 minutes.

Meanwhile prepare the Alabama white sauce. Place the mayonnaise and vinegar in a bowl and whisk together to combine. Add the salt, sugar, cayenne, fish sauce and miso and whisk again to combine. Set aside.

Once the wings are cooked through, remove them from the oven and let rest for 5 minutes. Place them on a large serving platter and cover them with the white sauce. Serve them with carrot batons.

nasi goreng with chicken thighs

No trip to Indonesia can be complete without sampling nasi goreng. This fried rice dish is everywhere and ranges from the sublime to the ridiculous. My version uses handmade basa gede, which is a spice blend common to many Indonesian recipes and which you'll see appearing time and again in this book.

For this version I use chicken thighs, which are roasted first and then sliced and fried again. The most important thing with nasi goreng is to fry the rice hard and then for a perfect finishing touch be sure to give a crispy edge to your fried egg. This is an ideal dish for breakfast, especially if you're planning some exercise later. And in my case, after two hours' surfing, it is all I need.

Use only vegetables for a vegetarian option – it's just as good.

SERVES 4

250g long-grain rice
8 chicken thighs
sunflower oil
6 large shallots, thinly sliced
4 tablespoons basa gede (see
    page 252)
1 carrot, peeled, quartered
    and thinly sliced
4 large eggs
1 tablespoon light soy sauce
5cm piece of cucumber,
    quartered lengthways
    and sliced
4 spring onions
sea salt and pepper

to serve
prawn crackers, to serve
    (shop bought is fine)
red chillies, sliced
cucumber, finely sliced

Cook the rice in boiling, salted water until just tender (15 minutes). Drain, rinse well, spread it out on a tray and leave to cool.

Preheat the oven to 200°C Fan (220°C/Gas Mark 7).

Lay the chicken thighs on a baking tray and season them on both sides with salt and pepper and a drizzle of sunflower oil. Cook for 20 minutes. Leave them to cool and then flake the flesh into large pieces; discard the bones.

Heat a little sunflower oil in a frying pan over a medium-high heat. Add the chicken meat to get it crispy and golden brown and then set aside.

Pour sunflower oil into the same frying pan to a depth of 1cm. Add the shallots and fry over a medium heat until crispy and golden brown. Lift them out with a slotted spoon and leave to drain on kitchen paper.

Spoon 2 tablespoons of the remaining oil into a large wok and heat it until smoking hot. Add the basa gede and stir-fry for 2 minutes. Add the cooked rice and carrot, and stir-fry over a high heat for another 2 minutes, until it has heated through. Add the fried shallots and the chicken thigh meat and stir-fry for another minute. Check the seasoning and add more soy, if necessary.

Fry an egg for each person and warm 4 large dinner plates in the oven.

Add the soy sauce, cucumber and most of the spring onions to the nasi goring and toss together well. Spoon on to the warmed plates. Top with the fried eggs and sprinkle with the remaining spring onions; serve straight away with the prawn crackers, chillies and cucumber on the side.

chicken skin nachos

These are a great, clever little canapé. The quince jam is well worth making yourself; however, if it all seems too much bother or if you're stretched for time, use shop-bought jam. Or simply buy some Membrillo/quince paste and add a little cider vinegar.

MAKES 250G

crispy chicken skins (see
    page 254)

for the quince jam
500g quince
500g sugar
juice of 2 lemons

Peel and core the quince, place them in 500ml water with half of the lemon juice, and cook for about 1 hour over a gentle heat.

Strain and chop the cooked quince. Transfer back to the pan, along with the sugar and remaining lemon juice and cook for another hour until it turns bright pink. Allow to cool and thicken.

Cut the chicken skins roughly into triangles, then add a dollop of quince jam on top – or just serve the triangles on a plate with a dish of the jam for dunking!

black pudding larp

This dish is a real show stopper!

Larp is the unofficial national dish of Laos, but thanks to migration into Thailand the Thais too have adopted this dish as their own. You know you've found a proper Thai restaurant when they have a blow-your-head-off larp on the menu. David Thompson's Long Chim restaurant in Perth is a particular favourite of mine; his larp uses chicken instead of the more commonly used pork.

In my search for the very best British produce to use in world cuisine, I think this variation of larp using black pudding is one of the most successful. The black pudding we use at the restaurant is from Stornoway, and is of wonderful quality and beautifully spiced. My larp is intensely hot with lots and lots of finger chillies and offers a lovely sweet, acid and sugary balance of fish sauce, lime juice and palm sugar. Quite often you find larp served with cabbage to cool the mouth, but for my version I substitute some dark green British winter kales or cavolo nero.

SERVES 4

250g black pudding,
   peeled and broken into
   small pieces
20ml vegetable oil, plus extra
   for the black pudding
25g long-grain rice powder
   (shop-bought or
   see method)
3 tablespoon nam pla
3 tablespoons lime juice
1 tablespoon palm sugar or
   brown sugar
3 bird's eye-chillies, sliced
2 banana shallots, sliced
1 lemongrass stalk, sliced
salt

to garnish
crispy shallots (shop-bought;
   or see page 253) (optional)
fresh coriander leaves
   (optional)
a few leaves of Thai basil
kale, cavolo nero or
   sweetheart cabbage
lime wedges

Preheat the oven to 200°C Fan (220°C/Gas Mark 7).

Cook the black pudding, drizzled with a little vegetable oil, in the oven for 20–30 minutes.

While the black pudding is cooking, make the dressing. Mix the nam pla, lime juice and sugar in a small pan, then dissolve the sugar over a gentle heat. Set aside until ready to use.

If you need to make the rice powder, simply pound in a mortar with a pestle until it is powdered.

Once the black pudding is cooked, transfer to a wok and stir-fry until it starts to crisp and the fat is rendered a little. Add the vegetable oil, chilli, shallots and lemongrass to the black pudding and stir-fry for a few minutes. Now add the dressing and rice powder and cook until the liquid is soaked up by the black pudding (30 seconds). Season to taste with salt.

Place in a bowl and garnish with crispy shallots, coriander, basil, kale and lime on the side to cool the mouth a little. This should be hot!!

starters & canapés

charred broccoli, broad beans, almonds and ranch dressing

It was in Hawaii that I first fell in love with ranch dressing, a simple mayonnaise-based sauce with garlic, buttermilk, soured cream and chives. The charring technique gives the broccoli a wonderful extra layer of flavour – a kitchen trick that works with pretty much any vegetable.

Blue cheese makes for a great addition to the dressing – melt 100g of Roquefort and add it to the mixture. Use this cheesy adaptation on Baby Gem salad leaves along with crispy bacon strips.

SERVES 4

1 head of broccoli
2–3 tablespoons olive oil
1 teaspoon sea salt
4 turns of freshly ground
    black pepper
2 garlic cloves, peeled but
    left whole
500g broad beans
75g flaked almonds
½ teaspoon butter
juice of ½ lemon

for the ranch dressing
150g mayonnaise
½ teaspoon red miso paste
75ml soured cream
2 garlic cloves,
    finely chopped
50ml buttermilk
½ teaspoon salt
1 tablespoon white
    wine vinegar
a handful of chives,
    finely chopped
a handful of parsley,
    finely chopped

Preheat the oven to 200°C Fan (220°C/Gas Mark 7).

First make the dressing: Mix all the ingredients together – except the herbs – until combined. Now stir the herbs through. Keep in the fridge until needed.

Cut off the broccoli stem and cut it into small pieces; break off the florets and slice in half to make smaller pieces. Mix 1 tablespoon olive oil and the salt, pepper and garlic cloves in a bowl. Add the broccoli pieces and stir to coat (stir in a little more olive oil if necessary). Place them on a baking tray and cook in the oven for around 10–15 minutes; then turn them over and cook for another 5–10 minutes until they are starting to brown and crisp. Keep an eye on them – depending on the strength of your oven they may brown very quickly.

While the broccoli is cooking, place the broad beans in a bowl, cover with boiling water for 1–2 minutes to soften them, then drain. Heat the remaining olive oil in a frying pan until hot, then fry the broad beans for about 5 minutes until crisp but not too browned.

In a dry pan toast the flaked almonds on a low heat until starting to colour. Add the butter and allow to foam for 30 seconds, then tilt the frying pan and spoon the foamed butter over the almond flakes. Remove from the heat and drain on kitchen paper.

Mix the broccoli and broad beans together and squeeze the lemon juice over; season with more salt if needed. Place in a bowl and top with ranch dressing and toasted almonds.

beetroot soup

This is a great winter vegetarian soup – simple and delicious. Salt-baking the beetroot concentrates the flavour and gives a great intensity to the mighty red root vegetable. The vegetable stock must be well flavoured with mushroom, lemon and star anise. The crispy shallots give a great texture, and the soup looks beautiful. This was actually one of my first dishes to make an appearance in the family business, sneaked in under the radar and on to the menu of our pub The Cornish Arms.

SERVES 4

500g raw beetroot, unpeeled
100g table salt, plus
   1 teaspoon
500ml vegetable stock
50g crème fraîche

to garnish
a few pickled shallots
   (see Jack's house pickle,
   page 257)
a handful of crispy shallots
   (see page 253)
a few chives, thinly sliced

Preheat the oven to 200°C Fan (220°C/Gas Mark 7).

Place the beetroot on a baking tray and cover it with the 100g salt, then bake it in the oven until a knife will pass easily through the middle (90 minutes). When cool enough to handle, wipe off the excess salt and peel the beetroot.

Heat the vegetable stock in a large pot. Add the beetroot and blitz with a hand blender until smooth. Season with salt.

Spoon into soup bowls and finish with a spoonful of crème fraîche.

Garnish the soup with the pickled and crispy shallots and the chopped chives.

summer tomato salad

There's not much to say about this perfect summer salad other than take care to use the very best tomatoes you can find, and don't put them in the fridge! I like to add salt to them before serving so that the juices come out.

I confess that I hate barbecuing – it's so often a time when people who don't normally cook and who can't cook are for some reason welcomed to cook. Leave the non-cooks to burn the sausages and murder the burgers and settle down to make this simple salad for everyone to tuck into while the massacre of the innocents takes place over fire and flame.

SERVES 4

400g heirloom tomatoes
1 ball burrata or mozzarella
    cheese (about 150g)
1 garlic clove, sliced
2 shallots, sliced crossways
2 tablespoons olive oil
1 tablespoons balsamic
    vinegar
a handful of basil
    leaves, sliced
sea salt and freshly ground
    black pepper

Slice the tomatoes and layer them over each plate; sprinkle with salt. Tear the cheese into chunks and place on top of the tomatoes.

Place the garlic and shallot slices in a microwaveable cup and cover with olive oil. Microwave on full power for 30 seconds–1 minute to confit the garlic and shallots. Allow to cool. Drizzle the oil, shallots and garlic over the tomatoes and cheese, and add a drizzle of balsamic vinegar. Sprinkle the basil leaves on top and season.

watermelon salad with feta and walnuts

This is what I take to a BBQ on those few hot, sunny days we get in the UK. It is based on the kind of salad you get in Australia all the time and inspired by my girlfriend, Lucy. It is simple and delicious – who could ask for more.

SERVES 4

½ large watermelon
125g rocket
a handful of walnuts,
    roughly chopped
50g pickled red onion
    (see Jack's house pickle,
    page 257)
200g feta cheese
a little extra-virgin olive oil
juice of ½ lemon
salt and pepper

Cut the watermelon in half and remove the rind. Slice the flesh into bite-sized cubes and place in a salad bowl. Add the rocket and mix together.

Place the walnuts in a dry frying pan over a low heat, allow to brown slightly for a few minutes, then turn off the heat and set aside.

Add the pickled red onion to the bowl and crumble the feta on top. Add the walnuts.

Drizzle over a little oil, add the lemon juice and season with black pepper and a pinch of salt. Stir to combine and serve.

oysters with lime juice and chervil

I first came across the combination of soy and mirin while working 'on stage', as a chef apprentice, at a restaurant in Sydney. They served oysters with finger limes, which are a very strange Australian citrus fruit. My own slightly adapted version uses ordinary lime juice in a savoury soy and mirin dressing and is garnished with chervil. With its acidity, the apple helps create a counterpoint to the salinity of the oysters.

Try to use the native European oyster for this dish – sweeter and fuller in flavour than the Pacific tear drop oyster and well worth the extra expense.

SERVES 4

12 oysters
3 tablespoons Japanese light
  soy sauce
2 tablespoons sake
3 tablespoons mirin
  (Japanese sweet rice wine)
1 tablespoon fresh lime juice
2 teaspoons sugar

to garnish
1 Granny Smith apple,
  peeled and cut into batons
12 sprigs of chervil
borage flowers

Place the oysters (make sure none have opened) in a pan with a tiny bit of water. Cover and steam for 1 minute. The shells should lift so that you can remove the top one.

Mix the soy sauce, sake, mirin, lime juice, sugar and 1 tablespoon water in a saucepan and warm over a low heat until the sugar has dissolved.

Making sure not to lose too much of their juice, serve the oysters in their shells, garnished with the apple batons, chervil and borage flowers. Pour over the lime and soy dressing.

razor clams with persillade butter

I love razor clams. Foraging for ingredients for the restaurant was something my brothers and I often did on weekends for pocket money – razor clams, winkles and mussels collected enthusiastically from the reefs around north Cornwall. Persillade butter made a big impression on me when I first had it served with gigantic mussels in Brittany. As with many of my recipes, this one incorporates some fond memories of food and travel brought together on a plate to make something new and delicious.

SERVES 4

12 razor clams
50ml vegetable oil
a little salt

for the persillade butter
2 tablespoons chopped chives
2 tablespoons chopped
   curly parsley
2 tablespoons
   chopped chervil
100g unsalted butter,
   slightly softened
I garlic clove
1 teaspoon lemon juice
3 pinches of salt

for the pickled shallots
150ml cider vinegar
25g sugar
1 tablespoon salt
2 shallots, thinly
   sliced crossways
2 sprigs of thyme
1 star anise
3 juniper berries
3 black peppercorns

to garnish
15g toasted pine nuts
12 borage flowers

Preheat the oven to 220°C Fan (240°C/Gas Mark 9).

To make the butter, blanch all of the herbs in boiling water for 20 seconds and refresh in a bowl of ice water. Drain off the water and put into a mixer. Cut the butter into chunks and add to the herbs along with the garlic; blitz until well mixed. Add the lemon juice and salt and blitz again to mix.

Wrap the butter in cling film to form a sausage shape (a ballotine) about 5cm in diameter and tie off the ends. Refrigerate for at least 1 hour, preferably overnight.

Meanwhile make the pickled shallots. Put the cider vinegar into a pan along with the sugar and salt. Add the sliced shallots, thyme, star anise, juniper berries and black peppercorns. Bring to the boil, then remove from the heat and leave to cool.

Now cook the clams. Into a saucepan with a lid pour water to a depth of about 1cm; bring it to the boil and immediately add the clams. Put on the lid and let the clams steam over a low heat for 3 minutes. Take the clams out of the pan and, when cool enough to handle, remove the clam from the shell.

Pan-fry the clams in the vegetable oil on one side until they are a light caramelised brown. Flip on to the other side for a quick flash fry over a high heat. Cut off the ends and the dark brown 'stomach'. Sprinkle a pinch of salt over them. Clean the shells with warm water and spoon the butter into them, then place the clams back on top. Place the shells on a baking tray and transfer to the oven for 1–2 minutes to melt the butter.

To serve, arrange 3 clams on each plate. Place a few pickled shallot slices on top of them and garnish with pine nuts and borage flowers.

razor clams with crab and samphire

This brilliant dish comes from Dan Hine, our sous chef at The Seafood Restaurant. Dan taught me how to cook on the mains section, which is the hardest section in the kitchen. It involves making the sauces and at the same time braising and cooking a lot of the fish. Dan is a real chef hero of mine, and a great teacher.

The simple sauce, made from stock, cream and butter with a little lemon juice, nicely sets off the sweet meat of the crab and the razor clams, all punctuated by the saltiness of the samphire harvested from the bottom of the estuary in Padstow.

SERVES 4

12 razor clams
200ml fish stock
 (see page 258)
200ml double cream
50g unsalted butter
80g white crab meat
100g samphire
2 teaspoons lemon juice
freshly ground black
 pepper

First tap the clams to make sure they are still alive; they should retract into their shells. Quickly rinse them in cold water. Fill a saucepan with water to a depth of 5cm, bring to the boil and drop the clams into it. Reduce the heat to medium, cover the pan and steam until the clams are partially cooked, about 2–3 minutes. Using your fingers or a sharp knife, pull the clams out of their shells. Set the clams and shells aside.

Pour the stock and cream into a saucepan and bring to the boil. Reduce until the sauce has thickened enough coat the back of a spoon (5–10 minutes). Stir in the butter to thicken the sauce further.

Next, add the razor meat and crab meat and heat through. Add the samphire, then the lemon juice. Season with black pepper.

Put the creamed shellfish back into the razor clam shells and serve.

xo clams

Whilst working at the world famous restaurant Tetsuyas in Sydney, after service we would often go to a classic Chinese restaurant called Golden Century. The restaurant has a cult following in Sydney and at that late hour would be filled with celebrities, the occasional ex-president or prime minister, chefs, bar people who had just finished shifts, serious drinkers and other dubious frequenters of late-night Sydney. One of the specialities at Golden Century is the XO pippies, a kind of Australian clam. The XO stands for 'extra-old', a sauce originally from Hong Kong. You can find ready-made XO Sauce online, but it is easy to make and well worth the little effort involved.

This is the sort of recipe that you can have fun adapting: try adding dried shellfish instead of fresh or amend the acidity in the dish – blood orange perhaps or grapefruit, instead of the lemon. Try XO sauce on other seafood, especially shellfish such as mussels, cockles or oysters. As in life so in cooking – have fun and never be afraid of experimenting.

SERVES 4

1 tablespoon vegetable oil
1 tablespoon finely
    diced ginger
1 tablespoon finely
    diced garlic
1 tablespoon finely
    diced chilli
800g clams
100ml dry sherry
25ml soy sauce
1 teaspoon lemon juice
a pinch of sugar

for the XO sauce
1 slice serrano ham, finely
    chopped
1 scallop (raw), minced
2cm piece of ginger
2 garlic cloves
3 red chillies, stems removed
    and deseeded
20g dried shrimp (optional)
2 tablespoons vegetable oil

to serve
a handful of spring onions,
    sliced on the diagonal

First make the XO sauce. Preheat the oven to 80°C Fan (100°C/Gas Mark low).

Place the ham and minced scallop on a baking tray and put into the oven until very dry (about 1–2 hours).

Mix them in a bowl with the ginger, garlic, chilli and dried shrimp.

Heat up the oil in a frying pan over a very low heat and cook the mixture in it for about 10 minutes, taking care not to let it colour. Set the sauce aside.

Now cook the clams. First heat the oil in a frying pan over a low heat and sweat the diced ginger, garlic and chilli for 2–3 minutes. Add the XO sauce and the clams and increase the heat. Add the sherry and cover the pan; cook for 1–2 minutes until the clams have opened (discard any that have not). Finally stir in the soy sauce, lemon juice and sugar.

Serve the clams with a dish of chopped spring onions alongside.

langoustine with pastis

Shellfish goes brilliantly with the aniseed flavour of tarragon, star anise, fennel and the much loved French spirit pastis. Amongst great British shellfish there is one that reigns supreme: the langoustine. And the langoustines from Scotland are the greatest of them all. They are expensive but well worth the money. If you can't get langoustines try using either tiger prawns, North Atlantic prawns, lobster or even crab. And now I'm thinking about it, this recipe would work very well with those pesky little American crayfish invaders that are becoming ever more common in British waters.

And if you are fortunate to come across a bottle of Tarquin's Cornish Pastis then your day and your dish will be made. In the last few years there have been many small distilleries opening across Britain producing gins and other spirits.

Tarquin's was the first British distillery to produce a French-style pastis. It is truly wonderful and in this dish, combined with the savouriness of the soy, the pungency of the mustard and the smokiness of the fish, helps to make the shellfish really sing.

SERVES 4

50g salt
8 fresh langoustines
2.5g dashi granules
    (½ sachet)
1 tablespoon extra-virgin
    olive oil
30g butter
2 handfuls of macadamia
    nuts
a small handful of tarragon
    sprigs, leaves only
salt

for the vinaigrette
1 shallot, thinly sliced
zest and juice of 1 lemon
1 teaspoon pastis

to garnish
5 nasturtiums, or other edible
    flowers, petals only
a small handful of salad
    leaves per portion

Add the 50g salt to 2 litres water and bring to the boil in a big pot. Add the langoustines and boil for 3 minutes. Drain and set aside.

In a small pan bring 200ml water to the boil; remove from the heat and stir in the dashi granules to dissolve. Set aside.

Add a dash of olive oil to a saucepan, along with a pinch of salt and the butter; then add the macadamia nuts to caramelise them. Cook over a medium heat until the nuts brown and the butter foams. Strain the liquid through a muslin cloth, then place the cloth on a flat surface and spread the nuts over it to cool. Transfer them to a chopping board; chop them roughly and set aside.

For the vinaigrette, place the shallot slices and the lemon zest and juice in a small bowl. Add the pastis and stir through.

Run a knife lengthways through each langoustine to split it in half. Lay the pieces face down on a hot grill pan and finish cooking on the heat for 1 minute. Remove the langoustines to a warm plate and quickly deglaze the pan with the dashi and pour this liquid into the vinaigrette. Mix well.

To serve, place 4 langoustine halves on each plate and drizzle a little vinaigrette over them, reserving some for the salad. Sprinkle the chopped macadamias on top, along with some tarragon leaves.

Place the salad of nasturtium flowers and salad leaves to one side and drizzle the remaining vinaigrette over this.

seared scallop succotash

This dish is nearly always on the menu at The Seafood Restaurant and I love it!

Succotash is a classic American dish consisting of sweetcorn, lima beans (similar to broad beans) and other ingredients which can vary depending on preference and tradition. It was a very common Great Depression dish owing to the frugality of the basic ingredients. It is often eaten at Thanksgiving in New England, so as an homage to the great American festival I have enhanced the original humble dish with some rather more festively celebratory ingredients – namely scallops, mussels and crab meat. My version omits the traditional lima beans. You can make the succotash without the shellfish (it will still be delicious), but they do help make it into something quite extraordinary.

SERVES 4

12 mussels
50ml dry cider
12 scallops, in the shell
25g butter
50ml double cream
60g white crab meat
salt and pepper

for the succotash base
50g butter
1 garlic clove, diced
2 shallots, diced
1 carrot, diced
1 leek, diced
1 celery stick, diced
1 (160g) can of sweetcorn,
    juice reserved
salt and pepper

to serve
a handful of finely
    chopped chives

To make the succotash base, place the butter in a saucepan and add the garlic, shallots, carrots, leeks and celery; cook over a low heat until soft but not coloured. Turn off the heat and stir in the sweetcorn. Season with salt and pepper and set aside.

Heat a pot until very hot, then add the mussels and cider; cover with a lid. After 1 minute check that all the mussels have opened (discard any that have not). Remove from the heat and drain. Remove the mussels from their shells and set all of them aside.

Take the scallops out of their shells (reserving these), and cook in a hot pan on one side only with the butter and a little salt. You want them to be nicely coloured. Turn them over, take the pan off the heat, and leave to finish cooking through in the residual heat.

Add a ladle of the juice from the sweetcorn and the double cream to the succotash base. Add the mussels (3 per portion) and the crab meat. Adjust the seasoning, if necessary, and cook until the succotash is thickened (about 1 minute). Replace the scallops in their shells and spoon the succotash, mussels and crab meat over them, scattering with the chives to finish.

scallops with truffle butter

I 'borrowed' this recipe from my time spent on a work placement in a lovely little restaurant called La Régalade in the 14th arrondissement in Paris. A man used to bring fresh truffles straight to the window of the kitchen, and the head chef, Bruno, would meticulously mince them for hours and then add them to softened butter. To this day, truffles remind me of my time in Paris.

I love cooking scallops in the shell; the roasting aromas that emanate from the baking shells just sing out and capture memories of beach barbecues.

If you are lucky enough to have some fresh truffle to hand simply substitute 200g of ordinary butter for the truffle butter, then shave the fresh truffle on top of the cooked scallops.

SERVES 4

12 scallops in their shells
a pinch of sea salt
1 tablespoon clarified butter

for the truffle butter

200g unsalted butter,
    softened, at room
    temperature
a large pinch of salt
10g truffle paste
1 teaspoon lemon juice

to serve

a handful of chopped chives,
    thinly sliced
a handful of crispy shallots
    (see page 253)
45g black truffle (optional)

First make the truffle butter. Mix all the ingredients together in a mixer fitted with the beater attachment, or you could do it with a hand mixer. Roll the butter into a sausage shape and chill until firm (or freeze it if you want it to last a while). This recipe will make more than you need, so freeze any leftovers.

Preheat the grill to high and the oven to 220°C Fan (240°C/Gas Mark 9).

When you are ready to serve, cut twelve 1cm slices of the truffle butter and set aside. Place the scallops on a baking tray, season with salt and drizzle a little clarified butter on top. Grill for 2 minute, then remove and place a slice of the chilled truffle butter on top of each scallop. Bake in the oven for a further minute until cooked (the scallops should be opaque and slightly browned).

Place 3 scallops on each plate. Sprinkle over the chives and crispy shallots and top with the shaved truffle, if using.

warm salad of new potatoes and st mawes hot smoked salmon

This dish is a healthy and colourful addition to any barbecue table. Salmon and horseradish are a match made in heaven, and the sweetness of Cornish new potatoes adds depth to what many people might think is just a simple salad. They would be wrong!

SERVES 4

400g new potatoes
200g mixed salad leaves, such as frisée and radicchio
400g smoked salmon
100g double cream
20g horseradish sauce
juice of 1 lemon
20g flat-leaf parsley, leaves only
salt and pepper

Cook the potatoes in salted water until tender. Let them cool slightly, then cut into 5mm slices. Put them in a mixing bowl along with the salad leaves.

Warm the smoked salmon under a grill or in a moderate oven for about 1 minute. Break it into chunks and mix it with the salad leaves and potatoes.

Lightly whisk the cream, horseradish sauce and lemon juice together using a hand whisk. It should start to thicken. Be careful not to over-mix; you want to keep it at a pouring consistency. Season with salt and pepper.

Combine all the ingredients together and garnish with parsley leaves.

raw salmon with pickled rhubarb and soy caramel

This is one of the dishes created during my time working on menu development for the Seafood Restaurant company. I had come across soy caramel in Australia once before, and we were just getting into what I call the 'pickle years', when we decided we would pickle everything that we could lay our hands on and then add them to as many dishes as we could find.

This dish is quite similar to a salmon tataki that you might find on a menu in Japan. The pickled rhubarb is very tart, complementing the sweetness of the soy caramel and the fattiness of the salmon. Use a good-quality organic farmed salmon, which has a higher-than-usual content of fat. You could substitute trout or sea trout here.

SERVES 4

400g salmon, skinned, filleted
   and portioned into 100g pieces
a little vegetable oil
4 slices of cucumber, 10cm
   long and 2mm thick (use
   a mandoline for this)
juice of 1 lime
a handful of finely
   sliced chives
1 tablespoon toasted
   sesame seeds
sea salt

for the pickled rhubarb
½ tablespoon fennel seeds
200ml rice wine vinegar
½ teaspoon chilli seeds
½ teaspoon salt
1 bay leaf
zest of ½ lime
½ tablespoon sugar
100g rhubarb, sliced
   2mm thick
30ml grenadine

for the soy caramel
1 (7g) pack dashi granules
1 tablespoon rice
   wine vinegar
1 tablespoon soy sauce
100g caster sugar

First pickle the rhubarb. Toast the fennel seeds in a frying pan over a medium heat until fragrant. Combine the vinegar, chilli seeds, salt, bay leaf, lime zest, sugar and fennel seeds in a saucepan and add 100ml of water. Warm the liquid and infuse the rhubarb for 5 minutes. then remove from the heat. Allow to cool and add the grenadine.

Next make the soy caramel. Begin by adding the dashi granules to the rice wine vinegar, soy and 40ml water. Stir to dissolve the granules and set aside. Make a caramel by heating a saucepan over a medium heat and slowly pouring in the sugar, stirring constantly. When the sugar has melted and has taken on a caramel colour, stir in the dashi liquid; set aside to cool.

Cover the salmon in a little vegetable oil and cook in a frying pan over a medium heat for 1 minute, so that it is still undercooked in the middle; the internal temperature should be 35°C.

Cook the cucumber slices in a dry frying pan over a medium heat until they are slightly coloured.

When you're ready to serve, use a pastry brush to add a line of the caramel to each plate. (If you're not feeling as fancy as that, just use a spoon!) Add a slice of cucumber across this, and top with a slice of salmon. Sprinkle the top with a little sea salt and a squeeze of lime juice, and place a spoonful of pickled rhubarb alongside. Finally scatter sliced chives and sesame seeds around the plate.

raw sea bass with apple and lemon verbena

Whenever planning a menu for a party, think of starting with a raw dish. You can get most of the recipe prepared in advance and just finish it when the guests arrive. This one is essentially a ceviche – a dish originally from Latin America based on raw marinated fish – but using British produce.

Lemon verbena is easy to grow and produces a delicious essential oil, often used in perfumery and cosmetics. The acidity in the cure pairs perfectly with the sweetness of the sea bass. The ponzu dressing delivers a full and flavoursome umami hit!

SERVES 4

200ml sunflower oil
40g verbena leaves
4 farmed sea bass fillets,
    between 80–100g each
2 Braeburn apples
sea salt

for the ponzu dressing
juice of 1 lemon
1 tablespoon rice wine
    vinegar
50ml Japanese soy sauce
2 teaspoons mirin
2g bonito flakes (about an
    espresso cupful)
1 sheet dried kombu, cut into
    1cm pieces

to garnish
12 chervil sprigs

Put the sunflower oil and verbena leaves into a blender and blitz until well combined. Strain through a sieve; discard the verbena leaves.

Now make the ponzu dressing. Mix all the ingredients together, leave for 24 hours in the fridge, then strain off the liquid and reserve. The dressing will keep for up to 6 months in the fridge.

Before serving, chill 4 plates.

Cut the sea bass into slices 2cm thick.

To segment the apples, first take a thin slice off the top and bottom and stand on a chopping board. Remove the core and cut the apple into quarters, then slice each quarter thinly.

Arrange the fish and apple slices on the cold plates and cover with the verbena oil. Splash with ponzu dressing, add a pinch of sea salt and garnish with the chervil.

st mawes smokehouse mackerel salad with apple and thai basil

I am not going to lie, this is pretty much the same as one of my father's recipes … but I have an excuse for including it. For one of his recent books he borrowed a couple of my recipes, so when I'd completed all but one of the recipes for my book and was wondering which to use for the last, I remembered how much I love this dish. I have changed just one ingredient to make it mine. At the restaurant we use green mango and papaya for this dish but because of the food miles travelled in order to get them I have substituted green apple, which has the same acidic quality. The smoked mackerel is delectable and oily, and packed full of healthy omega 3.

This can be as blisteringly hot as you want it to be – I like to add an extra bird's-eye chilli to the recipe when I make it at home. You could substitute different fish if you wanted; smoked trout works very well, as does hot smoked salmon. But for my money mackerel is the way to go – it's delicious.

SERVES 4, OR 2 AS A MAIN COURSE

4 smoked mackerel fillets
vegetable oil, for deep frying
½ Granny Smith apple
1 medium-sized carrot
   (about 75g)
60g very thinly sliced shallots
1 red bird's-eye chilli,
   finely chopped
25g roughly chopped
   roasted peanuts
4 teaspoons palm sugar
2 tablespoons fish sauce
about 2 tablespoons lime
   juice, depending on the
   tartness of the apple
15g roughly chopped Thai
   basil, roughly chopped

Skin the smoked mackerel fillets and break the meat into small flakes. Pour 2cm of oil into a pan and heat to 190°C, measured on a candy thermometer. Sprinkle the fish into the oil and deep-fry for 1 minute until crisp. The flakes will all stick together at this point, but don't worry. Lift them out on to a tray lined with lots of kitchen paper and leave to cool, then break up into small pieces again.

Peel the apple and carrot and shred, using a mandoline or shredder, into 3–4mm-wide strips. Put the apple, carrot, shallots, chilli, peanuts and fried fish pieces into a large bowl and toss together.

Mix the sugar with the fish sauce and lime juice until dissolved. Add it to the salad along with the Thai basil and toss together again.

Pile the salad on to 4 small plates (or 2 medium-sized plates, if serving as a main course), and serve straight away.

grilled mackerel fillets with pickled trerethern farm vegetables

Mackerel is probably my favourite fish – mainly because they are so easy to catch! There is something magical about dangling a line of feathers over the side of a fishing boat and pulling up masses of flapping mackerel. The sight of the mackerel flashing from the depths is something wonderful to behold.

As with a lot of oily fish, grilling is a great way to cook them. The oil in the skin helps to blister it producing big black and brown weals which taste delicious.

I've used shallot and carrot in this recipe but the vegetables can be whatever you can get. You can pickle almost anything, so add whatever you fancy to help cut through the oiliness of the mackerel.

SERVES 2

4 mackerel fillets
100ml rice wine or white
    wine vinegar
½ teaspoon dashi granules
    (optional)
1 small carrot (about 50g),
    thinly sliced
1 banana shallot, thinly sliced
2 juniper berries
2 black peppercorns
1 star anise
a sprig of thyme
a small pinch of chilli powder
a knob of butter
salt

to serve
1 tablespoon vegetable oil,
    plus a little extra
1 teaspoon capers
a few sprigs of chervil

Salt the flesh side of the mackerel fillets and leave them for at least 5 minutes.

Meanwhile, make the pickling liquid by combining the rice wine (or vinegar), dashi granules and 25ml water in a pan and warming gently over a low heat.

Wash the salt off the mackerel fillets and lay them in a shallow dish, skin side up. Pour over the pickling liquid, to the depth of the flesh but without completely submerging the fillets. Leave them to pickle for 10 minutes.

Remove the fillets from the liquid and pat dry. Reserve the pickling liquid and set aside.

Place the carrots and shallots in a pan with the juniper berries, peppercorns, star anise, thyme, chilli and a good pinch of salt. Pour the reserved pickling liquid over the vegetables, bring to the boil, then take off the heat and pickle for at least 10 minutes.

Meanwhile, heat the vegetable oil in a pan and fry the capers until crisp, then leave to dry on kitchen paper.

Preheat the grill to high. Season the mackerel fillets with salt and drizzle with a little vegetable oil. Place in a shallow baking tray and grill, skin side up, for 2–3 minutes.

Place 2 mackerel fillets on each plate, with some of the vegetables alongside. Deglaze the pan with 4–5 tablespoons of the reserved pickling liquid, reduce to a glaze, and drizzle over the plate. Garnish with capers and a few sprigs of chervil.

hake with curried sweetcorn

When I was working as a chalet chef in Switzerland I was forced to come up with lots and lots of canapés to feed the very hungry, party loving guests. Fiddly, fussy dishes are not really my strength but one day on chalet duty I came across some lovely hake in the local supermarket. After buying a few I went back and consulted Nikki Signit's brilliant and essential *Flavour Thesaurus*, where I learnt that hake goes very well with curry. So I set to and concocted a very simple curried sweetcorn purée. (If you have never made a purée before, sweetcorn is the easiest kind to start with.) Adding a tiny pinch of garam masala warmed it up and amazingly and it went perfectly with the hake.

So if you ever have the misfortune to need to make a canapé at any point in your life, make this one!

SERVES 8 AS A CANAPÉ

400g hake fillet
2 tablespoons vegetable oil
1 (198g) can of sweetcorn
25g unsalted butter
a big pinch of garam masala
salt

Slice the fish into bite-sized chunks and season with salt. Heat the oil in a non-stick pan. Fry the fish until golden (2 minutes). Dry on kitchen paper.

Warm the sweetcorn in a pan with the butter and half the liquid from the can, then boil for 5 minutes. Season with salt and garam masala. Put in a food processor and blend until smooth, then pass through a sieve. It should be the thickness of double cream. If necessary, warm again, as this should help to thicken it.

Serve the purée on spoons, with a chunk of the hake on top.

gin-cured trout with pickled cucumber

I came up with this dish after making my own gin in Margaret River, in Western Australia, whilst filming there for my TV series *Born to Cook*. Making your own gin is surprisingly easy. For mine I chose lots of flavours that reminded me of an English meadow, such as meadowsweet and chamomile – perfect accompaniments to the trout that you might find swimming in an English river.

I have used sea trout here rather than fresh water and cured it much as you would for gravadlax, with salt and sugar. It is quite Scandinavian in style with the pickle giving acidity and the grated horseradish adding a lovely heat.

Serve with some good wholemeal bread.

SERVES 6

1 side of sea trout or salmon
50g table salt, fine
1 pinch crushed white
    peppercorns
50g sugar
25g finely chopped dill
100ml gin

for the pickled cucumber
Jack's house pickle (see
    page 257)
1 cucumber

to garnish
a little fresh horseradish root
1 tablespoon fried capers (see
    page 102)

NOTE: Start this recipe the day ahead of serving; the trout needs to cure overnight.

Trim the 2 fillets off the bone and place one of them, skin side down, on a baking tray lined with cling film, then cover liberally with salt, white pepper, sugar and dill. Place the other fillet on the tray, also skin side down, and add salt and sugar. Douse both fillets liberally with the gin. Place one on top of the other, flesh sides together, and wrap the cling film tightly around them so that it is airtight, being careful not to let any of the juices escape. (If using salmon, slice the side of salmon in half and trim the belly, then continue with the instructions above.) Refrigerate for at least 24 hours.

Make the pickling liquid using the recipe on page 257. To prepare the cucumber, cut it in half lengthways, scoop out the seeds, then slice the halves into half moons 1cm thick. Add the cucumber slices to the pickle mixture, bring it to the boil, then turn off the heat and leave to cool.

To portion the trout, remove it from the cling film. Rinse the trout to remove and excess salt and thinly slice on an angle. Serve the slices on a plate and top with the pickled cucumber, horseradish and capers.

sardines with fermented ketchup

This slightly technical-sounding dish is in reality very simple to make. Fermentation is increasingly popular these days, and was something I first discovered while visiting Copenhagen some years ago. I was soon so keen that I even started a mushy pea miso, which I think is five years old now. It sits in the bottom of a cupboard, slowly doing its thing, and I check on it every six months. It is an acquired taste! This dish uses simple ingredients, including some store cupboard essentials that a lot of British chefs use more than most people would think: ketchup and Marmite! Technically the fermented part of the ketchup is the Marmite, if anyone asks!

SERVES 4

25g fennel tops, thinly sliced
50ml Jack's house pickle (see
    page 257)
2 tablespoons ketchup
½ teaspoon soy sauce
1 teaspoon Marmite
2 teaspoons butter
40ml (2½ tablespoons)
    chicken stock (see
    page 259)
a pinch of five-spice powder
8 butterflied sardines
    (a fishmonger could do
    this for you)
salt

to garnish
12 good sprigs of dill

Place the fennel and the pickle in a saucepan and bring to the boil, then turn off the heat and leave to cool.

Combine the ketchup, soy sauce, Marmite, butter, chicken stock and five-spice powder in another pan and bring to the boil, then remove from the heat and stir to emulsify.

Season the sardines with salt. Place them under a hot grill, skin side up, and cook for 1–2 minutes, then leave them to rest.

Place 2 sardines on each plate, along with the pickled fennel and fermented ketchup. Garnish with the dill sprigs.

venison carpaccio

This carpaccio is very simple and quite traditional except that the main ingredient is venison, not beef. The sauce is similar to the one served at Harry's Bar, in Venice, except that I incorporate some pickled beetroot. I created this recipe for my TV show *Born to Cook* using farmed venison, but I think wild venison, especially British, is far superior.

This is a perfect dish to start any dinner party because you can prepare it all in advance and just season and dress it at the last minute.

SERVES 4

400g loin of venison,
    chilled overnight
1 tablespoon butter
2 sprigs of thyme
a little extra-virgin olive oil
Maldon sea salt flakes
    and freshly ground
    black pepper

for the pickled beetroot

2 beetroots
Jack's house pickle (see
    page 257)

for the sauce

1 egg yolk
1 teaspoon white
    wine vinegar or red
    wine vinegar
2 pinches of dry mustard
170ml olive oil
juice of ½ lemon
1 tablespoon milk
1 or 2 dashes of
    Worcestershire sauce,
    or to taste
salt and freshly ground
    white pepper

to serve

25g Parmesan shavings
50g wild rocket

Place the beetroots on a chopping board and slice them into rounds 5mm thick. Add the beetroot slices to the cool pickling liquid and bring to the boil. Remove from the heat and set aside to cool, then store in a jar until required.

Sear the venison loin in butter, along with the thyme, in a hot pan until well coloured on the outside (3–4 minutes). Leave to cool, then wrap in cling film and place in the freezer for I hour, or overnight in the fridge.

Meanwhile chill 4 large plates.

Use a sharp knife to slice the meat into the thinnest possible slices. Lay the slices flat on a chopping board and cover them with cling film (you will need to do this in stages). Gently use a mallet to hammer them wafer-thin. Arrange the slices over the chilled plates, so that they cover the entire base, with the edges of the slices just butting up together, overlapping as little as possible.

Season the venison with salt and pepper and then drizzle over a little olive oil.

Now make the sauce, which is a variation of mayonnaise. First whisk the egg yolk and vinegar together until well blended, then add the dry mustard. Now start adding the olive oil, one small drop at a time, whisking as you go; take care that the mixture does not split. When it begins to thicken you can add larger drops of oil. When all the oil is incorporated, add the lemon juice, milk, white pepper and 2 shakes of Worcestershire sauce, and salt, to taste, if necessary.

Arrange the pickled beetroot over the carpaccio, drizzle the sauce on top and finish with shavings of the Parmesan and a little rocket.

guinea fowl terrine

I love guinea fowl, and this terrine is my favourite way of cooking it. We serve it in our restaurant in Marlborough, where our customers tend to appreciate and know a good terrine when they eat one.

This recipe comes from our head chef, Kevin Chandler. I love the combination of date purée and bitter salad leaves. Normally you get served a very sweet purée or chutney with a terrine, so this makes for a refreshing and welcome change. It has a lovely texture and sets off the bitter leaves perfectly.

Start this recipe a day ahead to give the terrine time to set.

**MAKES 1 TERRINE,
SERVES 15**

1 guinea fowl
1 tablespoon vegetable oil
2 chicken legs
100g streaky bacon, thinly
   sliced crossways
100g Parma ham
1 medium-sized onion,
   finely chopped
1 garlic clove, finely chopped
1 medium-sized carrot,
   finely diced
a sprig of thyme, leaves
   only, chopped
a sprig of rosemary,
   leaves only
1 teaspoon chopped parsley
50g unsalted butter
sea salt and freshly
   ground pepper

for the date purée
100g Medjool dates, pitted
1 garlic clove, peeled
a sprig of thyme

to serve
bitter salad leaves, about 50g
   per person
extra-virgin olive oil

Ask your butcher to break down the guinea fowl, removing the legs from the breasts, reserving the bones. Or you can do this yourself.

Preheat the oven to 180°C Fan (200°C/Gas Mark 6).

Place the guinea fowl carcass (including legs and wings) on a baking tray, season with 1 teaspoon of salt and rub with the vegetable oil. Roast the carcass until well coloured (20 minutes).

Put the carcass into a large pan and fill it with water to cover. Bring to the boil, then leave to simmer for 1 hour to make a stock. Strain off the liquid and reserve (discard the carcass).

Preheat the oven to 150°C Fan (170°C/Gas Mark 3).

Place the chicken legs in a deep roasting tin. Pour in enough stock to cover, reserving the rest, and braise the legs in the oven for 2 hours.

Once the chicken legs have cooked, strain off the stock and reserve. Transfer the chicken legs to a chopping board and flake off the meat.

Next, poach the guinea fowl breasts in the stock until they reach a temperature of 68°C, about 8 minutes. Reserve the stock and allow the breasts to rest for 10 minutes. Remove the skin and slice the breasts thinly lengthways. Put the flaked chicken leg and guinea fowl breast meat together in a single baking tray.

Get a large frying pan hot, cook the bacon over a medium-high heat until crispy, then add the onion and garlic. Cook, stirring occasionally, until caramelised. Add the stock and reduce to a glaze (30–35 minutes).

When it has nearly reduced to this point, stir in the carrots and herbs. Add the butter to the glaze and allow it to melt. Pour the glaze over the leg and breast meat. Season with salt and pepper. Line a terrine mould with cling film and fill it with the terrine; leave to set overnight.

The next day, release the terrine from the mould (the cling film makes this easy) and wrap the Parma ham around the sides.

Make the date purée. Place all the ingredients in a pan, cover with water and bring to a simmer. Gently simmer for 20 minutes. Then remove the thyme and purée in a blender (a stick blender can be used for this).

To serve, lay a slice of terrine on each plate and add about 2 tablespoons of purée alongside with the bitter leaf salad. Drizzle some olive oil over the leaves.

mains

truffle mac 'n' cheese

While on my way to begin filming for my TV series in Australia, I found myself sitting in an anonymous airport hotel in Singapore trying to finalise the recipes for the show. I had a list of ingredients to be used in the shoot and a list of recipes that I had in mind, but the thing I was struggling with was truffles. Now you may think that truffles are easy to cook with, and they do lend themselves to many sophisticated dishes, but for my show I really wanted to try to use the truffle in a simple, everyday dish.

In the end I decided to do mac and cheese, mainly because its rich creaminess lends itself so well to fresh truffles.

This dish needs lots of everything: lots of cream, lots of cheese and lots of truffle. Trust me, this is a winner.

SERVES 4

1 litre milk

a few sprigs of fresh thyme, leaves only

2 dried bay leaves

4 garlic cloves, peeled and roughly chopped

600g dried macaroni

100g butter

3 heaped tablespoons plain flour

1 teaspoon Dijon mustard

100g Parmesan cheese, grated

150g Cheddar cheese, grated

½ teaspoon dark soy sauce

2 splashes of Worcestershire sauce

1 teaspoon Marmite or Vegemite

a handful of panko breadcrumbs

sea salt and freshly ground black pepper

to serve

some shaved truffle or 1 teaspoon truffle oil

Preheat the oven to 180°C Fan (200°C/Gas Mark 6).

Pour the milk into a saucepan and warm it to just below a simmer over a medium-low heat. Drop in the thyme, bay leaves and garlic, then turn off the heat, leaving them to infuse.

Meanwhile, bring another pan of water to the boil, add the macaroni and cook until al dente (6 minutes or as stated on the packet). Drain it in a colander.

Now make a blond roux. Melt 60g butter in a pan and then add the flour. Stir well over a low heat until the flour is cooked out – that is, until it is no longer visible (2–3 minutes). Strain off the hot milk (discard the garlic and herbs), then slowly add the milk to the roux, whisking to remove the lumps. A stick blender is best for this. Add the mustard, Parmesan and Cheddar, stirring until melted through. Add the soy sauce, Worcestershire sauce and Marmite or Vegemite. Season to taste then fold the macaroni into the sauce, and pour it into an ovenproof dish.

Melt the remaining butter in a pan and stir in the breadcrumbs so they are nicely coated. Layer them over the top of the macaroni and bake in the oven for 20–30 minutes or until the breadcrumbs are browned.

Shave the fresh truffle over the top and serve. Or pour a little truffle oil over each serving.

green pasta bits

This is a dish from my girlfriend, Lucy, who is from a Sicilian family. Lucy usually makes this on a Monday, when we have a ton of uncooked green vegetables left over from preparing the Sunday roast. You can use virtually any green vegetable. Be sure to leave the Parmesan rind in the pasta to give it a lovely depth of flavour. If I have been busy at work and really want something comforting and healthy to eat, this is it.

Once when I was working at The Seafood Restaurant, an Italian woman was invited into the kitchen. While I was showing her around, she told me that the best way to cook pasta was her way. So here it is. Cook the pasta as usual, then, when it's ready, drain it through a colander, being careful to collect the water in a pan. Add butter to the hot pasta, stir it through and pour the water back through the pasta again. This is the way I have cooked pasta ever since!

SERVES 4

3 tablespoons olive oil plus
  more if needed
1 onion, finely chopped
½ teaspoon chilli flakes
2 garlic cloves, finely
  chopped
100g grated Parmesan
  cheese and Parmesan rind
500g dried rigatoni or penne
400g mixed green vegetables,
  such as fresh tenderstem
  broccoli, asparagus and
  spinach, and frozen peas
  (used here)
1 tablespoon butter plus an
  extra knob for the pasta
juice of ½ lemon
salt and pepper

Fill a pan of water for the pasta. Salt generously and bring to the boil.

Heat the olive oil in a large pan over a medium heat, add the onion and chilli flakes and a pinch of salt, and cook slowly until soft but not coloured (about 5–10 minutes). Add the garlic and the Parmesan rind. Leave on the lowest possible heat while you prepare the rest of the dish.

Meanwhile add the pasta to the boiling water and cook until al dente, about 1 minute less than the packet instructions suggest.

Prepare the vegetables. Slice the broccoli stems and asparagus spears into 2cm pieces, keeping the heads intact. Add them to the pan containing the onion mixture, and turn up the heat, stirring so that they are covered with oil. Add 1 tablespoon butter and a pinch of salt. Cook for 5 minutes until they are softened but still have a bite.

Wash the frozen peas under warm water to defrost them; drain off the water and add the peas to the broccoli and asparagus and cook for 1 minute. Cut the spinach into strips and add to the pan; let it wilt down and add another pinch of salt. There should be enough oil to coat all the vegetables; if necessary, add a little more.

When the pasta is ready, drain it into a colander set over a large pan. Put the pasta back into the pan and stir through a knob of butter. Pour the collected water back into the pan to coat the pasta and drain over the large pan again.

Remove the Parmesan rind. Pour in the vegetable sauce and stir to make sure it is all combined. Add the lemon juice and a handful of Parmesan and stir these through, along with a final tablespoon or two of the pasta cooking water.

Plate up the pasta and vegetables and top with more Parmesan, black pepper and a drizzle of olive oil.

maple-roasted pumpkin with rocket, dukkah and feta

I love pumpkin and as my birthday falls on Halloween it's perhaps natural that I would share an affinity with it. It's often a struggle to devise light dishes at this time of year but this great autumnal vegetarian salad fits the bill perfectly. Dukkah is a North African combination of seeds, spices and nuts and works brilliantly with the sweetness of the pumpkin and the sourness of the feta.

SERVES 4

1 pumpkin
2 tablespoons maple syrup
2 tablespoons olive oil
½ teaspoon chilli flakes
50g shelled walnuts
60g hazelnuts
1 tablespoon cumin seeds
40g pumpkin seeds
40g sesame seeds
1 teaspoon pepper
100g feta cheese, crumbled
3 teaspoons sea salt

to serve
150g rocket
juice of ½ lemon
some crusty bread with extra-
    virgin olive oil for dipping

First prepare the pumpkin. Peel it and then, using a large, heavy knife, cut the pumpkin in half. Using a spoon, scrape out the seeds and fibres. Finally, using a sturdy vegetable peeler, remove the outer skin. Cut the flesh into cubes about 2cm in size.

Preheat the oven to 200°C Fan (220°C/Gas Mark 7).

Put the pumpkin cubes in a bowl, along with the maple syrup, 1 tablespoon olive oil and the chilli flakes. Season with 1 teaspoon sea salt, and stir to coat.

Transfer the coated pumpkin cubes to a large pan (one that will fit into the oven) and cook over a high heat to colour them, turning until golden brown (about 5–10 minutes). Now put the pan in the oven to continue cooking for 20–30 minutes.

Meanwhile, make the dukkah. In a dry frying pan cook the walnuts and hazelnuts on a low heat until toasted. Add the cumin seeds and cook for another few minutes until toasted. In a food processor blend the nuts and cumin seeds quickly to roughly break them up then transfer to a bowl.

In the same dry frying pan, toast the pumpkin seeds until they are brown and beginning to pop, then toast the sesame seeds for 30 seconds. Stir the pumpkin and sesame seeds into the bowl with the walnuts, and add 2 teaspoons of salt and 1 teaspoon pepper.

During the last 5 minutes of the pumpkin-cooking time, sprinkle the feta on top, then return the pan to the oven.

Remove the pumpkin from the oven and allow to cool a little.

Transfer the roasted pumpkin and feta to a bowl and stir to mix. Add the rocket and toss together. Drizzle with the remaining tablespoon of olive oil and squeeze over the lemon juice. Add more salt if necessary.

Add half the dukkah and mix through. Serve the salad in bowls with extra dukkah alongside and some crusty bread and extra-virgin olive oil.

chickpea and quinoa falafels with garlic yoghurt and salad

When I think about falafels I'm reminded of the first
time I ate one – Glastonbury 2002. Falafels are the
perfect festival food as they are light and flavoursome
and make you feel semi-healthy after all the ordeal you
have put your body through. It's not surprising then
that these days, purveyors of juice bars and falafels do
a roaring trade at festivals around the globe! But you
don't have to go to a festival to enjoy these wonderful
treats as they make for a lovely, healthy lunchtime
meal – the warmth of the spices balanced against the
earthiness of the salad.

To make the falafels vegan, simply omit the egg
and cheese and dress with olive oil only.

SERVES 4

1 (400g) can of chickpeas,
    drained
2 garlic cloves,
    finely chopped
2 spring onions,
    finely chopped
1½ teaspoons ground cumin
½ teaspoon paprika
a pinch of cayenne pepper
1 small carrot, grated
a handful of grated Cheddar
    cheese (optional)
1 tablespoon plain flour
1 egg, beaten (optional)
100g quinoa, cooked
    according to packet
    instructions
1–2 cups of breadcrumbs
    (depending on whether the
    egg is used)
a small bunch of parsley,
    finely chopped
1 teaspoon each salt and
    pepper, plus a little
    extra salt
vegetable oil for frying

for the dressing
230ml Greek yoghurt
1 garlic clove, very finely
    chopped
1 tablespoon finely
    chopped chives
juice of ½ lemon
a little olive oil
...

Drain the chickpeas and blend quickly in a food processor to break them up roughly. Place in a bowl along with the garlic, spring onions, spices, carrot and grated cheese (if using) and stir through. Sprinkle the flour over and mix together. Add the egg and quinoa and mix together, using your hands.

Now add the breadcrumbs. Start with half a cup and mix this through; if the mixture is too wet, add another half cup, then, if necessary, a little more. Stir in the parsley and the salt and pepper.

Form the mixture into balls and flatten out gently to make falafel shapes. Put on a plate, cover and put in the fridge for 10–20 minutes so that the falafels bind well and will not break up when frying. You can make these in advance and leave them in the fridge until needed; they will keep for 1 or 2 days.

Now make the dressing. In a bowl mix the yoghurt, garlic and chives. Squeeze in the lemon juice and drizzle with olive oil. Stir and refrigerate until needed.

Prepare the pepper for the salad. First roast it with the skin on. If you have gas elements, turn on high heat and put the pepper directly on to the flame, so that the skin blisters and blackens. Alternatively put it in the oven (180°C Fan [200°C/Gas Mark 6]) for 15 minutes until the skin blisters. Run the pepper under hot water and place in a plastic bag, then rub the bag against the pepper: this will remove the skin easily and contain the mess.

Once the skin is removed, cut out the core at the top, slice the pepper in half and scrape out all the seeds. Slice into long strips and place in a bowl with 1 tablespoon olive oil and a pinch of sea salt flakes.

Remove the falafels from the fridge. Pour the olive oil into a frying pan to a depth of 2cm and turn the heat to medium-high. Place the falafels in the pan and cook for about 3–5 minutes on each side until golden brown and warm through. To check, cut one in half; if it is not warm in the centre, cook the falafels for another 2 minutes until golden brown and cooked through. Drain on kitchen paper and season with a little salt.

...continued on page 127

for the salad

1 red pepper
1 tablespoon olive oil
a pinch of sea salt flakes, plus
  more if needed
100g spinach
100g rocket
100g feta cheese (optional)
50g kalamata olives, halved
  and pitted
a small handful of shelled
  pistachio nuts
½ lemon

In a bowl mix together the spinach leaves, rocket leaves, feta (if using), olives, roasted pepper strips and oil. Break up the pistachios roughly and toast in a dry pan for 1–2 minutes. Add to the salad. Squeeze over the half lemon and season with salt.

Plate the salad up and add the falafels on top. Drizzle the yoghurt sauce over and enjoy!

saffron barley risotto

This luxurious risotto is the perfect partner for osso bucco (see page 194) and the piquant parsley oil gremolata provides the finishing touch. Pearl barley requires a longer cooking time than traditionally risotto rice, but the mascarpone cheese gives the unctious feel that normally comes from the risotto rice starch.

SERVES 4

1.25 litres vegetable stock
   (see page 258)
2 tablespoons olive oil
1 onion, finely chopped
2 garlic cloves, crushed
Parmesan rind, plus 60g
   Parmesan cheese, finely
   grated
250g pearl barley, rinsed
200ml dry white wine
50g mascarpone cheese
a big pinch of saffron
salt and pepper

for the parsley oil gremolata

a handful of finely chopped
   parsley
2 garlic cloves, finely
   chopped
zest and juice of 1 lemon
1 tablespoon extra-virgin
   olive oil

Pour the vegetable stock into a deep pot and bring to the simmering point over a medium heat. Turn the heat down to low and leave the stock to keep warm.

In another deep pot, place the olive oil, onion, garlic and Parmesan rind; season with salt. Stir together over a medium-low heat until softened but not coloured (about 15 minutes). Add the rinsed barley to this pot and turn up the heat. Stirring constantly, to prevent it from catching, cook the barley for about 1 minute.

Add the white wine and allow to evaporate. Now begin adding the stock, one ladleful at a time, stirring each one in until almost absorbed before adding the next. Continue this process until all the stock has been incorporated and the barley is cooked al dente. Remove from the heat, stir through 50g of the Parmesan and the mascarpone and saffron, and cover to keep warm.

Now make the gremolata. Put the parsley, garlic, lemon juice and olive oil in a bowl; mix together and season with salt.

Just before serving, remove the Parmesan rind. Spoon the risotto on to individual plates and top it with the parsley oil gremolata. Sprinkle with some lemon zest and a little extra grated Parmesan and serve.

mussels with miso and black beans

The key to cooking mussels, in my opinion, is the shells. I love the smells you get the world over from mollusc shells being cooked on street stalls and in far flung kitchens. The shells help give a wonderful depth of flavour to the finished dish. I remember once having clams a la plancha in San Sebastian and wondering what ingredient in the sauce gave them the wonderful smoky flavour. I asked the barman and he said 'nothing' – it was just the combination of a hot griddle and the scent of the shells. For this recipe you want everything to be red-hot and done in seconds. Make sure to give the shells a good fry in the oil before adding the savoury elements. The interaction between savoury ingredients, such as the miso and the soy sauce, and the sweetness of the mussels produces a perfect balance.

SERVES 4

1.75kg mussels
1 teaspoon Chinese salted
   black beans
¼ teaspoon sugar
3 spring onions
2 tablespoons groundnut oil
4 garlic cloves, finely
   chopped
15g fresh root ginger, peeled
   and finely chopped
1 teaspoon brown miso
1 tablespoon dark soy sauce
2 tablespoons Chinese rice
   wine or dry sherry
3 tablespoons fish stock
   (see page 258)
1 tablespoon chopped fresh
   coriander

First clean the mussels. Fill the sink with water and add the mussels; move them around in the water – dirt will fall to the bottom. Place the mussels in a colander and run water through them; shake them a bit. Discard any that are open after being in the water and that don't close when tapped on the counter.

Rinse the black beans, then place them in a bowl; add the sugar and mash together.

Trim the spring onions and cut across them to separate the white part from the green. Thinly slice both sections and place in separate bowls.

Put the groundnut oil in a wok or large, deep frying pan, with a lid, and heat until very hot. Add the mussels, and stir-fry until you smell the smokiness of the shells, about 1 minute.

Now add the garlic, ginger and black beans and stir-fry for about 30 seconds, until the smell of hot ginger and garlic rises. Add the white of the spring onions and stir-fry for a few seconds. Now add the miso, soy sauce, rice wine or sherry, and stock. Cover and steam the mussels open for about 3–4 minutes.

Add the coriander and the green spring onion, toss together and serve with some toasted sourdough bread for dipping in the sauce.

lobster with chips

This dish has a story! Let's just get the fundamentals established first: we are blessed with the best lobsters in the world from the North Atlantic, bar none. Today, serving lobster with chips is considered perfectly normal, but back in the early 1990s things were different. My father had recently been commissioned to do his first series for the BBC and to celebrate he brought back two things that we never usually saw at home: a lobster and a bottle of 1987 Ampeau Montrachet (a beautiful bottle of white Burgundy from one of the best vintages of the 1980s). He proceeded to knock up a meal of lobster, chips and Montrachet. A combination that would have been frowned on back then by many, but to me it exemplifies his blithe disregard for what people think and his love of simple things. This sublime combination of food and drink is, for me, up there with sherry and iberico ham.

SERVES 4

4 (500g) cooked lobsters
4 tablespoons clarified butter
150ml fish stock (see
    page 258)
100g butter, cold and cubed
juice of ½ lemon
a handful of tarragon leaves,
    roughly chopped
salt

for the chips
500g Maris Piper
    potatoes, peeled and sliced
    into 2cm-thick batons
sunflower oil for deep frying
salt

to serve
some mixed salad leaves
a few lemon wedges

First prepare the chips. Rinse the potatoes in water to remove the starch. Immerse them in boiling water for 6 minutes, then drain and dry them on kitchen paper. Now double-fry them in the sunflower oil: first at 140°C for 4 minutes (leaving to cool afterwards), then at 180°C until crisp and golden. Season with salt.

Preheat the grill so that it is hot. Cut the lobsters in half and season with salt; pour over the clarified butter and place the lobsters on a grill tray. Cook under the grill for 8–10 minutes until cooked through; the internal temperature should have reached 68°C. You may need to do this in batches; if so, keep the cooked lobsters warm on a plate under foil.

For the sauce, heat the stock, let it boil, then whisk in the cold butter until emulsified. Finish with salt, the lemon juice and tarragon. Scoop out the cooked head meat and anything left on the grill tray and put it into the sauce.

Serve the lobsters and chips with a green salad. Drizzle the sauce over the salad and lobsters.

crispy soft-shell crab salad with peanut chilli sauce

We get soft-shell crabs for just a few glorious weeks in the summer, brought in to us by a great local forager called Taff. We have had them on the menu for years. One of the joys of the soft-shelled crab is that you can eat the whole thing, shell and all.

But the good news is that you don't have to have a Taff to hand as these crabby delights can be ordered on-line all the year round. They can be expensive, however, so if you cannot source them just use some white crab meat to top the salad instead, as it works just as well with this delicious peanut chilli sauce.

This dish was originally created by one of our Australian chefs and is wonderfully fresh and vibrant. Make the batter at the last minute and be sure to use very cold, previously unopened soda water.

SERVES 4

for the peanut chilli sauce
50g tamarind pulp
3 medium-heat red chillies
50g ginger, peeled
75g peanuts, roasted
½ head of garlic,
   cloves peeled
35ml rice wine vinegar
25ml ponzu or lime juice
2 tablespoons vegetable oil

for the salad
3 lemongrass stalks
2 kaffir lime leaves
a bunch of coriander,
   leaves only
4 spring onions, thinly sliced
1 red chilli (mild, medium
   or hot, according to
   taste), sliced
1 tablespoon sesame oil
1 teaspoon lemon juice
100g cornflour
100g plain flour
a good pinch of sea salt
soda water, ice cold
12 soft-shell crabs

First make the peanut chilli sauce. Extract the juice from the tamarind pulp by soaking it in a little warm water and then mix it with your hands and push it through a sieve. If it is too solid to push through the sieve, add a little more water. Place the extracted tamarind juice in a blender or food processor along with the remaining sauce ingredients and blitz until well combined. (Discard the leftover tamarind pulp.)

For the salad, remove and discard the outer layers of each lemongrass stalk to reveal the heart; slice this thinly. Now chiffonade the kaffir lime leaves by placing one on top of the other and roll them up tightly. Hold the roll on a cutting board and, using a sharp knife, slice the roll at an angle to produce thin ribbons. Add these to the lemongrass slices, then add the coriander leaves, spring onions and chilli. Dress with the sesame oil and lemon juice.

Stir together the cornflour and plain flour and add the salt. Whisk in enough soda water to make a thick, lumpy batter. Coat the soft-shell crabs with the batter and deep-fry at 180°C until golden brown (3–4 minutes). Drain on kitchen paper.

Serve the salad with the crabs on top and peanut chilli sauce on the side.

crab shangurro

Shangurro – or, as the Basques call it, txangurro – is a dish, usually made with spider crab, traditionally served in the Basque homeland on the north coast of Spain. I first ate this in San Sebastián, which really has become one of the gastronomic capitals of the world. There are famous food destinations, like Tokyo, that I haven't properly explored yet and others that are close to my heart, but none come close to San Sebastián. It's a chef's dream: multiple two- and three-star restaurants, nestled in amongst the most amazing pintxo bars – streets and streets of them!

If you can lay your hands on some spider crabs then you are in luck: if not then use brown crab. Serve them in the shell and enjoy this wonderful celebration of Basque cuisine whilst using a great British product.

SERVES 4

3 tablespoons olive oil
2 onions, finely chopped
8 garlic cloves, finely
   chopped (1 kept separate)
225g plum tomatoes,
   chopped
100ml dry white wine
1 teaspoon caster sugar
¼ teaspoon dried chilli flakes
450g white crab meat
100g brown crab meat
50g white breadcrumbs
2 tablespoons melted butter
3 tablespoons chopped flat-
   leaf parsley, plus a little
   for serving
salt and pepper

Heat the oil in a heavy-based pan. Add the onions and the larger amount of chopped garlic and sweat gently until soft.

Increase the heat and add the tomatoes, wine, sugar, chilli flakes and salt and pepper to taste. Simmer until the mixture has reduced to a thick sauce. Remove from the heat.

Stir in the crab meat and transfer to a large, shallow baking tray. Leave to cool.

Mix the breadcrumbs, butter, parsley and remaining garlic together and spread this over the top of the crab mixture. Place the dish or tray under a grill, set at low, to brown on top, around 30 seconds or so.

Serve the shangurro in empty crab shells, if you have them, or in shallow bowls, and scatter with some extra parsley.

lemon sole with griddled lettuce and a soft-boiled duck egg

This dish came about from a collaboration with Ross Geach, the ex-chef turned farmer who supplies our restaurant with vegetables. We did a 'one-mile-meal', showcasing what could be grown and caught within a mile of our restaurant. (I think this is a bit tongue in cheek because we can't make mustard or Parmesan within those constraints; however it was a good way to get thinking about using what was available locally.) Ross had a lot of duck eggs at the time, so we decided to include those. The original dish used flounder, which are plentiful in the Camel estuary, but here we've used lemon sole, though any flat fish, such as plaice, would work well.

SERVES 4

2 duck eggs
100g piece of Parmesan
    cheese
a little oil for the griddle pan
2 Baby Gem lettuces,
    halved lengthways
2 (350–450g) lemon
    sole, filleted
25g butter, melted
Maldon sea salt flakes
    and freshly ground
    black pepper

for the mustard vinaigrette
3 teaspoons English mustard
3 teaspoons cider vinegar
80ml rapeseed oil
salt and pepper

Pre-heat the grill to high.

Cook the eggs in boiling water for just 6 minutes so that the yolks remain slightly soft. Cool, peel and cut in half.

Using a sharp potato peeler shave some thin slices off the piece of Parmesan cheese; set aside.

For the mustard vinaigrette, mix the mustard and vinegar together in a small bowl and then gradually whisk in the rapeseed oil so it thickens. Season to taste with some salt and pepper.

Warm 4 large plates in the oven.

Heat a ridged cast-iron griddle pan over a high heat. Brush with oil, then place the lettuce halves diagonally across it and grill them for slightly less than 1 minute on each side, so that they get nicely marked with diagonal lines. (Add a little more oil to the pan if the lettuce is looking too dry.)

Remove the lettuce from the griddle pan and arrange it in the centre of the warm plates.

Cut each sole fillet diagonally across into two similar-sized pieces. Brush on both sides with the melted butter and season well with salt and pepper. Lay the fillets, skin side up, on a lightly greased baking tray or the rack of the grill pan and grill for 2–3 minutes.

Sprinkle each fillet with a little coarsely crushed black pepper and some sea-salt flakes. Place a lettuce half, a duck egg half and a couple of Parmesan slices alongside. Stir 1½ teaspoons warm water into the mustard vinaigrette and drizzle this around the plate.

sea trout with samphire and beurre blanc

For as long as I can remember, we have used samphire and a few other wild foods in the restaurant. There is something amazing when in late May the first samphire, the seafood lover's asparagus, comes in from the estuary. But now that these wild food ingredients are so popular and plentiful, produced in quantity in hydroponic greenhouses, we can easily get them all the year round. The saltiness of the samphire goes beautifully with the sea trout and its beurre blanc sauce. You can substitute salmon or freshwater trout.

SERVES 4

zest of 1 lime
zest of 1 lemon
1 tablespoon sea salt
4 (200g) sea trout fillets
4 teaspoons vegetable oil

for the beurre blanc

4 banana shallots, finely
  chopped
50ml dry white wine
50ml white wine vinegar
50ml water or fish stock
  (see page 258)
200g butter, cold and cubed
50ml double cream
1 teaspoon salt

to serve

200g samphire
black pepper to taste

Mix the lime and lemon zest with the salt and rub this over the trout fillets. Allow to cure for 30 minutes–1 hour, then wash off the citrus-salt mixture.

Pat the trout dry with kitchen paper and heat the vegetable oil in a frying pan. Cook the fillets in the oil, skin side down, over a medium heat until the edges and the undersides become opaque. Now flip the fillets over and take the pan off the heat. The residual heat should give you an internal temperature of 45°C. The colour inside should be nice and pink.

For the beurre blanc, place the shallots in a saucepan and add the wine, vinegar and water or stock. Cook over a medium heat, allowing the liquid to reduce until it completely evaporates, leaving only the shallots. Then slowly whisk in half of the cubes of cold butter. Add the cream and continue whisking while adding the rest of the butter. Bring the sauce to a simmer and allow it to bubble and thicken. Season with salt.

Just before serving, place the samphire in a pan with a splash of water and season with pepper (not salt, as it is already salty). Cover the pan and steam the samphire over a high heat for 1–2 minutes.

Divide the samphire among 4 serving plates, top with the trout and serve the beurre blanc sauce alongside.

hot and sour sumatran soup with sea bass

As I am sitting here typing this introduction, I'm about to go back to Krui, in southern Sumatra. There is not much there – just a small town and a famous beach club called Mandiri, run by a group of legendary Englishmen who set it up on the very edge of the jungle.

Close to the camp I found a restaurant where the chef serves the best fish-head soup you will ever try. Surprisingly it contains cherry tomatoes, though less surprisingly it is blisteringly hot. Fish heads are like chicken wings to me: cheap and so very tasty. Eating them is messy; you have to be diligent and dig out every bit of the meat from the skull – trust me, it will be well worth it.

Use any fish you fancy though sea bass are probably the easiest to find. If you can't face dealing with fish heads, though I would urge you to try, you can leave them out and simply add more fillet.

SERVES 4

4 sea bass heads
20 cherry tomatoes
12 Thai green finger chillies
4 fillets of farmed sea bass,
    each cut into 3 pieces
fish sauce, to taste
the juice of 1 lime
a few sprigs of Thai basil

for the Asian chicken stock

1kg chicken wings or 4
    chicken carcasses
50ml vegetable oil
5 shallots
50g ginger, peeled and sliced
6 lemongrass stalks, bruised
100g tamarind paste
2 garlic cloves
1 star anise
50g galangal (optional)

to serve

1 cucumber, thinly and
    diagonally sliced

First make the stock. Colour the chicken wings in the oil in a frying pan until nicely browned. Then add 2 litres water and the other ingredients. Simmer for 2 hours until reduced to 1 litre, skimming off the fat occasionally. Remove from the heat and allow to cool.

Pass four-fifths of the stock through a fine sieve into a fresh pan and bring it to a simmer (discarding the leftover stock). Add the fish heads, cherry tomatoes and chillies; reduce the heat to a low simmer and cook for 5 minutes. Add the fish fillets and cook for another 5 minutes, then probe the cheeks and heads with a meat thermometer; they should have reached 55°C.

Meanwhile warm 4 soup bowls in the oven.

Place a fish head and 3 pieces of fillet in each soup bowl, along with the stock, cherry tomatoes and chillies. Taste the soup and season it with fish sauce and lime juice; finish with a few leaves of Thai basil.

Serve the soup with the sliced cucumber alongside.

hake with winter salad

We were filming a Christmas special for the BBC and a winter fish salad was urgently needed. Under pressure the creative juices began to flow and I figured that a take on a Christmas wreath would go down well. So I picked my colours – the reds and dark greens – and looked towards beetroots, pomegranates and dark green winter leaves. This recipe is the result. I think it looks spectacular and makes a great first course at Christmas.

SERVES 4

6 medium-sized beetroots,
    peeled
a pinch of caster sugar
1 strip of lime zest
1 strip of lemon zest
2 cloves
2.5cm piece of cinnamon stick
100g red cabbage,
    finely shredded
100g green cabbage, such as
    hispi, finely shredded
100g white cabbage,
    finely shredded
50g kale or cavolo nero,
    finely shredded
a small bunch of
    chives, chopped
a small handful of fennel fronds
1 tablespoon sea purslane
    leaves (optional)
a small bunch of sea beet leaves,
    finely shredded (optional)
4 (100g) pieces of hake fillet
25g butter
50ml dry white wine
100ml fish stock (see page 258)
sea salt flakes

for the dressing

3 tablespoons beetroot juice
    (from the cooked beetroots)
2 tablespoons cider vinegar
3 tablespoons rapeseed oil
½ pomegranate, seeds only
salt

Place 2 of the beetroots in a small pan with the sugar, a good pinch of salt, the lime and lemon zest, and the cloves and cinnamon. Cover with cold water, bring to the boil, lower the heat and leave to simmer very gently for 1 hour or until tender when pierced through to the centre with a fine skewer. Remove the cooked beetroots and set them aside to cool.

Meanwhile, roughly chop the 4 remaining beetroots and blend in a food processor to a smooth purée. Tip the purée into a sieve set over a bowl and press out all the liquid with the back of a spoon or a spatula. This should yield about 75ml of liquid. Set this aside for the dressing.

Cut 1 of the cooked beetroots into thin slices, then cut these into fine matchsticks. Mix the shredded cabbages, chives, fennel fronds, beetroot matchsticks and the sea purslane and sea beet (if using) together in a large bowl. Set aside. Season the hake on both sides with salt and set aside for 10 minutes.

Meanwhile, for the dressing, whisk the beetroot juice with the vinegar, oil and some salt to taste. Set aside.

To cook the hake, first melt the butter in a non-stick frying pan large enough to hold the fish comfortably side by side. Pat the hake dry with kitchen paper, add to the pan, skin side down, and cook over a medium-high heat until pale golden brown (1–2 minutes). Turn the pieces over, add the white wine and fish stock to the pan, cover and cook for another 2–3 minutes, until cooked through. Keep warm.

To finish the dressing, whisk 2 tablespoons of the cooking liquid from the fish pan into the beetroot dressing and season to taste with salt. Add 4 tablespoons of the dressing to the cabbage salad and mix until well combined. Stir the pomegranate seeds into the remaining dressing.

To serve, thinly slice the remaining cooked beetroot and overlap the slices to form a disc in the centre of each serving plate. Place a 10–12cm cooking ring in the centre of a beetroot disc and fill with the salad mixture. Carefully lift the ring off and repeat for each of the remaining plates. Place a piece of fish on top of the salad and spoon the dressing and pomegranate seeds around to finish.

trash of turbot

A few years ago I was looking closely at how we could reduce the waste from the restaurants. This included looking at parts of animals or plants that we normally discard when preparing our dishes and seeing how we could treat them in new ways and make them delicious. The 'Trash of Turbot' came from this exercise by utilising both the turbot cheeks and also the burnt butter solids produced when clarifying butter for pan-frying the fish. We then looked at farm produce and started to play with left-over roots and stems of vegetables such as beetroots and turnips. And then I remembered the amount of oil that renders out of our chorizo, so we whacked that in too. The resulting recipe is a complete waste … but in the best possible way.

SERVES 4

5 beetroot stems
Jack's house pickle (see
    page 257)
2 tablespoons sunflower oil
12 turbot (or other
    fish) cheeks
20g butter
100g unsalted butter, melted
3 tablespoons skimmed
    milk powder
250ml double cream
½ teaspoon salt
1 teaspoon lemon juice

to serve

50g turnip or other green
    veg tops (i.e., the bits you'd
    normally discard, such as
    outer leaves)
1 tablespoon chorizo oil, left
    from cooking chorizo (or
    vegetable oil infused with
    red chilli flakes)

Pickle the beetroot stems following the instructions on page 257 and reserve.

Heat the sunflower oil in a large frying pan over a medium heat and cook the cheeks for 1 minute on each side. Add the 20g butter, flip the cheeks over again and cook for another 30 seconds. Note that you will need to cook the cheeks in batches; as each batch is finished, transfer them to a warmed plate and leave to rest.

Melt the unsalted butter in a saucepan and add the milk powder; cook over a medium-high heat, stirring continuously, until it goes brown and nutty. Remove from the heat and add the cream. Leave to steep for 10 minutes then pass through a fine sieve into a saucepan.

Bring the sauce to a boil and let it bubble till it thickens (about 5 minutes). Stir in the salt and lemon juice.

Serve the cheeks with the drained pickled beetroot stems, waste tops such as turnip or sprouts and the brown butter sauce. Finish with a drizzle of chorizo oil.

turbot on the bone roasted with bone marrow sauce

Turbot is, as far as I'm concerned, the best luxury fish available anywhere. And the best way of cooking this King of the Sea is on the bone. By keeping the fish on the bone you retain so much moisture during cooking and, as with cooking meat on the bone, it adds great flavour. (If you can't source turbot, I suggest using a thick piece of cod, for example.)

Here I have paired the turbot with an unctuous bone marrow gravy, something more usually associated with a steak. Add some truffle to make this the most voluptuous fish dish imaginable.

SERVES 4

4 (250g) pieces of turbot
    on the bone
45ml vegetable oil
100g butter
4 sprigs of thyme
salt and pepper

for the bone marrow sauce
500ml beef stock (see
    page 259)
25g unsalted butter
50g shallots, peeled and
    thinly sliced
75ml white wine
1 teaspoon soy sauce
1 teaspoon Worcestershire
    sauce
1 teaspoon Dijon mustard
5ml sherry vinegar
5ml lemon juice
50g bone marrow, rinsed
    and diced
a handful of chives

to serve
a little shaved truffle or some
    truffle oil (optional)
new potatoes (optional)
your favourite green veg
    (optional)

Preheat the oven to 200°C Fan (220°C/Gas Mark 7).

Pour the beef stock into a small saucepan and reduce over a high heat to about 100ml (one-fifth the original quantity).

Meanwhile melt the butter in a frying pan and fry the shallots until light brown. Add the wine, soy sauce and Worcestershire sauce and reduce to about 2 tablespoons. Remove the pan from the heat and stir in the mustard, sherry vinegar and lemon juice. Stir in the reduced beef stock.

Bring the sauce back to the boil, then remove from the heat and add the diced bone marrow. Finely chop the chives and add to the sauce.

Season the turbot pieces with salt and pepper and fry them in the vegetable oil (in batches if necessary) over a medium-high heat until coloured on both sides. Place them on a baking tray, add the butter and thyme, and bake in the oven for 8–10 minutes. Check the temperature near the bone; it should be 55°C. Leave the turbot to rest on warmed plates.

Serve the turbot with the sauce – adding, if you like, some shaved truffle on the top or a drop of truffle oil on each portion.

Serve with new potatoes and greens.

brill tail with spring vegetables and miso

In 2010 I had completed some work experience at Michel Bras, the legendary three-Michelin-star restaurant in Laguiole, southern France, a town otherwise famous for its steak knives. I was so impressed by the way they handled vegetables to make their signature gargouillou – one of the world's best looking dishes made with a profusion of fresh vegetables, cooked with a little ham to deepen the flavour – that I set out to create something similar. I wanted to add some body to it, so added a little sweet white miso – an ingredient I had first seen used in a sauce at the wonderful Tetsuya's Restaurant in Sydney. So in essence I was combining two great kitchens – French and Japanese – into one.

SERVES 4

80g peas (fresh or frozen)
50g asparagus: 4 spears cut
    into 5mm slices
1 large courgette (around
    100g), cut into 5mm cubes
2 tablespoons vegetable oil
4 brill tail fillets (approx.
    120g each)
60g butter
40g iberico ham

for the lemon confit
15g lemon zest
35ml lemon juice
1 teaspoon sugar

for the white miso
chicken stock
200ml chicken stock (see
    page 259)
1 teaspoon white miso

to garnish
a few pea shoots (optional)

To make the lemon confit, place all the ingredients in a small pan over a low heat and bring up to around 75°C. Leave to simmer for 30 minutes. Set aside.

In the meantime make the white miso chicken stock. Simply warm the chicken stock over a low heat, then add the white miso and stir to mix. Keep warm until ready to use.

Bring a pan of water to a boil and blanch the peas, asparagus and courgette for 30 seconds.

Heat the oil in a frying pan and add the brill, skin side down. Cook the brill for 1–2 minutes, or until it reaches 45°C when a meat thermometer is inserted into the thickest part. Add 20g butter to the pan and baste the brill.

To make the ragout, put the ham into a saucepan and cook over a medium-low heat for 30 seconds to render the fat. Add the vegetables and sauté for 30 seconds. Finally add the stock and cook for 1–2 minutes, until the vegetables are cooked through.

To finish, finely dice the lemon confit. Then melt the remaining butter and allow to foam. Stir in a pinch of the diced lemon confit.

To serve, place a brill tail on each plate, add the ragout, and garnish with the lemon confit and pea shoots.

pollock fillet with tartare sauce, new potatoes and spinach

If I'm ever asked what my all time favourite meal was I plump for this. Some friends and I went pollock fishing one summer and returned successful to a friend's house to make lunch. With simple and cheap ingredients we settled down at my friend Munch's table and enjoyed the most delicious meal imaginable. To this day I still think there's nothing quite like eating and being amongst friends, having caught or picked all the ingredients with your own hands and then cooked them for the communal table, accompanied with plentiful bottles of good wine as the day drifts lazily on. As I recall, after several glasses of wine, I proclaimed it the best meal I'd ever eaten. I still think, despite all the places I've visited and meals I've eaten in my life, this remains the highlight.

SERVES 4

800g pollock fillets
1 tablespoon vegetable oil
500g spinach, washed
1 teaspoon butter
400g new potatoes, boiled
salt and pepper

for the tartare sauce
150g miso mayonnaise (see page 252)
½ shallot, finely chopped
25g capers, chopped
25g gherkins, chopped
½ tablespoon chopped tarragon
½ tablespoon chopped chives

First make the tartare sauce. Place the miso mayonnaise in a bowl and add the shallots, capers and gherkins. Mix them until well incorporated, then stir in the tarragon and chives. Refrigerate until needed.

Season the flesh side of the pollock fillets, and oil lightly. Grill, skin side up, under a hot grill for 2–3 minutes, depending on the thickness of the fillets. Set aside and allow to rest for 2–3 minutes. Sauté the spinach in the butter until wilted.

Serve the pollock fillets with a large dollop of tartare sauce and with the potatoes and spinach alongside.

cod with chard and charred sweetcorn dressing

I developed this dish after Ross, the farmer who supplies our restaurants, said he'd planted a lot of rainbow chard. The cod is sweet and flaky, the chard is earthy and the sweetcorn dressing has lots of savoury notes to complement the sweetness of the fish. Charring the sweetcorn gives extra depth of flavour, so either use a blowtorch or just chuck it under the grill. This dish looks as pretty as a picture.

SERVES 4

4 cod fillets with skin on
(180g each)
2 teaspoons sea salt, plus
more as needed
30ml vegetable oil
a knob of butter
200g chard, cut diagonally
a drizzle of olive oil

for the corn vinaigrette
2 ears of sweetcorn
1 tablespoon sunflower oil
1 teaspoon sea salt
1 banana shallot, minced
1 teaspoon English mustard
a sprig of thyme
50ml cider vinegar
200ml extra-virgin olive oil
a pinch of garam masala
1 teaspoon dark soy sauce

Season the cod fillets with sea salt. Heat the vegetable oil in a non-stick frying pan to a medium heat and cook the fillets skin side down for 2–3 minutes until the tops of the fillets begin to change to white in colour (this method allows the skin to brown slowly). Add a knob of butter to the pan, flip the fish, turn off the heat and leave the fillets to finish cooking in the residual heat. Check the temperature with a probe; it should read 50°C. Once the fillets have reached this temperature, remove them from the pan and leave to rest. Do not clean the pan; set it aside to use later.

Meanwhile, make the corn vinaigrette. Husk the sweetcorn and cut the kernels from the cobs. Place the kernels in a bowl, along with the sunflower oil and 1 teaspoon salt, and toss to coat. Transfer to a baking tray, place under a hot grill, on the middle shelf, and grill for about 15 minutes, turning occasionally, until the kernels start to blacken. (Or use a blowtorch for this.)

Place the minced shallot in a bowl. Add the mustard, thyme, cider vinegar, extra-virgin olive oil, garam masala and soy sauce, and stir together. Then add the charred sweetcorn to the mixture and stir. Set the vinaigrette aside.

Put the pan used to cook the fish back on the heat. Deglaze the pan with 2 tablespoons water, then add the corn vinaigrette to warm it up. It should take 1 minute.

Place the chard leaves in a saucepan along with water to a depth of 5cm. Cover the pan with a lid and steam the chard over a high heat for 1 minute. Once wilted, add salt and olive oil to taste. Remove from the heat.

Divide the chard among 4 plates, dress it with the vinaigrette and place the cod fillets on top.

shredded chicken thighs with cornish new potatoes and spring greens

This is a very economical dish with spring greens and chicken thighs being such good value. Chicken thighs are full of flavour and this way of cooking brings out the very best in them. Five-spice powder goes well with poultry in general and it gives a special boost to the flavourful chicken thigh meat.

The star here, though, is the humble potato. It really sings when roasted with the chicken thigh meat, the sweetness accentuated by the meat juices in the same way that roast potatoes do in a traditional British Sunday lunch.

SERVES 4

6–8 chicken thighs, skin on
1 tablespoon olive oil
a large pinch of five-spice
    powder
400g new potatoes
500g spring greens or other
    dark vegetable such as kale
    or cavolo nero
25g butter
salt and pepper

Preheat the oven to 200°C Fan (220°C/Gas Mark 7).

Cover the thighs in the oil and season with salt and pepper. Roast on a baking tray in the oven for 25 minutes until well browned. Take them out and leave to rest for 20 minutes. (Leave the oven turned on.) When slightly cooled, pull the chicken apart with a fork and remove all the meat from the bone. Season with the five-spice powder and set aside to cool. Drain off any excess fat (tip the roasting pan over a container until the fat has flowed off the top), but keep the meat juices. The bones can be reused for stock.

Place the potatoes, unpeeled, in 1 litre of salted water; bring it to the boil, then simmer until they are soft (20 minutes). Drain and set aside.

Slice the spring greens into 2cm-thick strips. Put a little water in a saucepan. Add the greens and cover; this will steam them but keep them from going soft and losing their flavour and nutrients. Keep the pan covered for 2–3 minutes, adding more water if necessary. Add the butter and toss the greens to mix it in.

Slice the potatoes about 2cm thick and place them in the tray with the cooking juices and shredded meat. Put them back in the oven for 5–6 minutes to warm.

Serve the chicken and potatoes together with a portion of spring greens. Finish with a little sprinkle of five-spice powder and salt.

whole butter-roasted chicken

Take one very good-quality free-range chicken and insert an absolutely monumental quantity of butter inside its cavity and then roast it – perfect!

A roast chicken is one of the hardest things to get right. There are so many different bone and muscle densities within the bird and each bird requires a slightly different approach to cooking time and temperature. To compensate for this, I like to brine my chicken, as this softens the muscles and makes for more succulent meat, and then I roast my chicken at a very high temperature initially and then drop it to 120°C Fan and cook it for longer than normal. This enables the breast and thigh to settle down and even out.

The chicken butter that comes out of the bird should be kept in the fridge and can be used for cooking other dishes – a great way of making one joint go a very long way.

SERVES 4

1 whole chicken (about 1.4kg
    in weight)
1 whole garlic bulb
125g butter, chopped
    into large chunks, plus
    50g softened
a sprig of thyme
freshly ground black pepper
4 shallots, peeled (3 cut in
    half, 1 diced)
1 teaspoon sugar
4 teaspoons cider vinegar
1 teaspoon English mustard
1 teaspoon honey
1 hispi cabbage, cut into
    quarters and outer leaves
    removed (optional)
vegetable oil
Maldon sea salt and freshly
    ground black pepper

to serve
roast potatoes (see page 248)

First brine the chicken. Place it in a large pot or basin and pour in enough water (measured) to cover it. Add 100g salt for each litre of water and leave for 2 hours.

Towards the end of the brining, preheat the oven to 220°C Fan (240°C/Gas Mark 9). Remove the chicken from the brine, rinse away the salt and pat dry; transfer to a roasting tin.

Cut the garlic bulb in half crossways (leaving it unpeeled) and insert it into the chicken cavity. Add the 125g of butter and the sprig of thyme into the cavity. Rub the 50g softened butter all over the chicken skin and season it with 10 turns of freshly ground pepper. Place the 3 halved shallots around the chicken and sprinkle them with the sugar.

Roast the chicken for 45 minutes, then lower the temperature to 120°C Fan (140°C/Gas Mark 1) and baste it. Leave it for 1¼ hours, and test it for doneness: the internal temperature should be 70°C or more, and if you pierce a drumstick with a fork the juices should run clear. Remove the chicken from the oven and let it rest for 30 minutes. Transfer it to a carving board.

For the vinaigrette, pour the chicken juices into a bowl (first skimming off any fat with a spoon), along with the diced shallot; add the cider vinegar, mustard and honey, and stir together.

If you are serving with cabbage, place a griddle pan over a high heat. Rub the cabbage quarters all over with salt and vegetable oil. Grill them on the hot pan, pressing them down on each cut side for 3 minutes, using a spatula or tongs, then for 1 minute on the outer side. Place the grilled cabbage halves on a platter, cut side up, and pour ¾ of the vinaigrette over them.

Carve the chicken and serve it with the grilled cabbage, roasted shallots and roast potatoes. Dress each serving with the remaining chicken vinaigrette.

carl's chicken clusters in laksa sauce

This is one of Carl Clarke's dishes. Carl has been
a friend of mine for many years; he is a very creative
chef and a lovely man. He has set the chicken world
alight with his Chick'n'Sours restaurants, and now his
CHIK'N looks like being another success. I owe him
a lot as he helped formulate the idea of using British
produce in a global context, an ethos which underpins
this book.

   In this recipe chicken thighs are coated in panko
breadcrumbs and served with a laksa sauce. The idea
of going to Singapore or Penang Road, in Malaysia,
and sitting down for a laksa just makes me so happy.
The flavours are intense, and this is a particularly
good version.

...continued on page 164

SERVES 4

for the laksa paste

2 large dried red medium-heat
  chillies
2 lemongrass stalks
1 teaspoon shrimp paste
1 tablespoon dried shrimp,
  soaked in water until soft
50g small round shallots, peeled
1 teaspoon finely chopped
  galangal
4 garlic cloves, peeled
25g macadamia nuts
½ teaspoon coriander seeds
½ teaspoon cumin seeds
½ teaspoon ground turmeric
½ teaspoon salt

for the laksa sauce

20ml vegetable oil
300ml coconut milk
1 tablespoon palm sugar
1 tablespoon fish sauce
juice of ½ lime

for the chicken clusters

25g flour
½ teaspoon salt
1 egg, beaten
5 teaspoons whole milk
100g panko breadcrumbs
4 boneless, skinless chicken
  thighs, diced into 1.5cm
  pieces (about 400g in total)
vegetable oil, for deep frying

to serve

a small handful of crispy shallots
  (see page 253)
a small handful of pea shoots
a few red chillies
200g cooked rice vermicelli

For the paste, soak the dry chillies in cold water for 1 hour, then drain.

Remove the tough outer layer from the lemongrass and discard. Roughly chop the remainder and the soaked chillies, then place them in a blender with all the other paste ingredients. Purée until smooth.

To make the sauce, first heat the vegetable oil in a frying pan over a medium heat, then add the paste. Sauté, while stirring, until caramelised and aromatic (about 7–8 minutes). Add 300ml water, coconut milk, palm sugar and fish sauce, then bring to a simmer. Gently cook for 5 minutes, then squeeze in the lime juice. Turn the heat down low to keep the laksa sauce just warm while preparing the chicken clusters.

Have ready 3 medium-sized bowls. Combine the flour and salt in one bowl; in another bowl mix together the egg and milk; in a third bowl place the panko breadcrumbs.

Pour the vegetable oil into a saucepan deep enough to cover the chicken clusters (or use a deep fryer if you have one) and heat to 185°C. Use a sugar thermometer to check the temperature (or use the fryer's temperature control), or drop a small piece of white bread into the oil; it should be golden brown after 30 seconds.

Now, working in batches of several chicken pieces at a time, coat the pieces to prepare them for frying. First add them to the seasoned flour; mix, then toss to completely coat each piece. Remove the pieces from the flour, shake off the excess, then drop them into the egg mix. Tip them into a sieve to drain off the wet batter (discard the excess batter). Finally add them to the breadcrumbs and use your hands to coat each piece thoroughly. Place all the battered chicken pieces on a plate.

Have ready a baking tray lined with kitchen paper. Now, working quickly, with one chicken piece at a time, carefully drop each piece into the hot oil and cook for about 2½ minutes until golden on the outside. Once cooked, use a slotted spoon to transfer the cluster to the tray; the kitchen paper will soak up any excess oil.

To finish, divide the laksa sauce among 4 shallow bowls. Add the cooked rice vermicelli. Add 1 serving of chicken clusters to each bowl, then sprinkle some crispy shallots and pea shoots on top. Garnish with a few red chillies.

pork belly with burnt lettuce and apple sauce

Sometimes less is more, and this is definitely the case here. This is a dish with just three components, each treated relatively simply, complementing each other beautifully. Admittedly, brining the pork belly takes some time (10 hours), but, as with some other joints, chicken and turkey for example, this really is essential; it achieves a lovely soft 'mouth feel' in the finished dish.

Chargrilling lettuce is a simple way of adding a more robust flavour, making it a suitable partner for the pork. And apple sauce is, well, apple sauce.

...continued on page 167

SERVES 4

1 pork belly, trimmed of
   fat and skin (trimmed
   weight 800g); bones
   removed but reserved
2 apples, cored and chopped
20g sugar
1 tablespoon five-spice
   powder
1 tablespoon butter
4 baby cos lettuces, halved
   lengthways
a little vegetable oil
sea salt

for the brine
200g salt
2 garlic cloves, crushed
1 tablespoon white
   peppercorns
3 bay leaves
2 star anise

NOTE: Your butcher should be willing to trim the fat and skin from the joint; alternatively you can do this yourself. Using a small, flexible knife, cut through the fat but not into the flesh – you should be left with a smooth white top. Reserve the trimmed skin for the crackling.

First make the brine. Pour 2 litres water into a large pot or basin, then add the salt, stirring until dissolved. (For brining, generally, the proportion of salt to water is 10 per cent – here, 200g salt to 2 litres water.) Add the garlic, peppercorns, bay leaves and star anise. Immerse the pork belly in the brining liquid and place the pot in the fridge; leave it refrigerated for 10 hours.

Remove the meat from the brining liquid and rinse off the excess salt. Transfer it to a large cooking pot along with the star anise and bay leaves.

Fill the pot with water to about twice the depth of the pork and add the bones for flavour. Bring the pot up to the boil over a high heat, then quickly drop it to a low simmer. Leave the meat to cook for about 3 hours.

Remove the pork from the stock and place it between 2 baking trays; place weights, such as cans of food, on top to flatten the meat. Chill in the fridge for 1 hour.

Meanwhile make the apple sauce. Place the apples in a saucepan with 20g of sugar and a ladleful of the simmering pork stock. Leave them to bubble for 10 minutes, then purée with a stick blender. Return the apples to the pan and add the butter; stir to mix. Set aside.

Preheat the oven to 190°C Fan (210°C/Gas Mark 7). Place a heavy baking tray in the oven to heat, and begin making the crackling. Season the skin with lots of table salt on both sides and let it sit for 30 minutes. Rinse off the excess salt and pat dry. Score the skin into your desired pattern, put on the pre-heated baking tray and roast for 25 minutes.

Take it out of the oven and lay another baking tray on top of the crackling to weigh it down. Return to the oven for 30 minutes to crisp. Once the crackling is cooked, remove the baking trays from the oven and set aside.

Remove the pork from the fridge and cut into 4 portions then sprinkle with some of the five-spice powder and salt. Finish the pork in the frying pan with the tablespoon of butter, spooning it over the pork until it is starting to brown and caramelise, about 3 minutes. Transfer the pork to the oven and finish cooking for 10 minutes.

Just before serving, brush the cut sides of the lettuce with a little vegetable oil. Place them, cut side down, on a hot griddle pan and lightly char them. Season with a pinch of five-spice and sea salt.

Assemble the pork, lettuce and apple sauce on plates and serve with the crackling alongside.

babi galung

This is one of those dishes that, to be honest, will probably taste great however you make it. All over Bali you find little *warungs* (roadside restaurants) selling this dish. Unusually, for such a savoury feast, it is traditionally eaten in the morning. Some of the best versions of this are from Ubud, in the uplands of Bali.

As with all such things, when you hear of a secret version of a classic dish you just have try to seek it out … and so it was that I and one of our head chefs set out on mopeds at 4am driving around the rice paddies having read that the only way to find this secret babi galung was to follow our noses! We were told that workers would be streaming past the restaurant before their day's work in the fields, but alas, we did not find it, could not smell it and ended up on the beach at Canggu eating a cheese and tomato toastie as the sun rose!

I use pork shoulder for my version of babi galung and it is imperative that you brine it before cooking, as this softens the meat and makes it so much more unctuous.

SERVES 4

2kg pork shoulder, boned

for the pork rub
2 tablespoons turmeric
1 tablespoon salt

for the pork seasoning
4 shallots, chopped
1 lemongrass stalk, chopped
2cm ginger, peeled
5 medium-heat chillies
1 teaspoon salt
3 garlic cloves
1 teaspoon black pepper
2 kaffir lime leaves
2 tablespoons vegetable oil
juice of 1 lime
7 macadamia nuts

for the peanut salad dressing
2 tablespoons peanut butter
1 tablespoon kecap manis
2 tablespoons vegetable oil
juice of 1 lime
2cm ginger, peeled
1 chilli
1 garlic clove
a pinch of salt
1 lemongrass stalk, chopped
100ml coconut milk

to serve
400g fine green beans,
   topped and tailed
2 tablespoons crispy shallots
   (see page 253)
400g rice, cooked
4 kaffir lime leaves,
   finely sliced

First brine the pork in a 10 per cent brine, as described on page 167. This is best left overnight.

The next day, prepare the pork rub. Mix together the turmeric, salt and 2 tablespoons water and rub it all over the pork shoulder. Leave to marinate for 2 hours.

Preheat the oven to 200°C Fan (220°C/Gas Mark 7).

Place all the pork seasoning ingredients in a food processor and blend until combined. Add the mixture to the inside of the pork shoulder, then roll it and tie it to hold the stuffing in place. Transfer the stuffed pork shoulder to a deep-sided baking tray and pour about 700ml water around it.

Roast the pork for 20 minutes, then reduce the heat to 160°C Fan (180°C/ Gas Mark 4) and cook for a further 4–5 hours. Check occasionally to make sure there is still liquid in the bottom of the baking tray, and add more water if necessary. When fully cooked the pork should be soft and easy to pull apart if you insert a knife and press to one side. If it is still tough, put it back in the oven for another hour.

Take the pork out and let it rest for 20 minutes. Pour any cooking juices into a pan and cook over a medium heat until thickened and reduced.

For the dressing, combine all the ingredients except the coconut milk in a blender (or use a stick blender). Pour the mixture into a saucepan, and heat on a medium heat for 2 minutes. Add the coconut milk and cook for another 2–4 minutes until warm and slightly thickened. Pour into a bowl and refrigerate until needed.

Just before serving, boil the beans in slightly salted water for 4 minutes, then place in cold water to stop the cooking process. They should still have a slight bite to them. Place the beans in a bowl and top with the peanut dressing and crispy shallots.

Place the pork on a big board and carve and pull it into portions. Pour over some of the reduced cooking juices and stir together to coat. Serve the pork with the bean salad and rice scattered with the crispy shallots and lime leaves.

pork cheeks with celery, basil oil and meat vinaigrette

This is a dish inspired by my time working at La Régalade, a tiny bistro in the 14th arrondissement in Paris. One of their signature dishes was pork belly served with a kind of basic pesto. The combination of freshness from the basil oil and the flavour heft of the meat juices works so well.

Pork cheek is a bit like pork belly: when cooked it falls apart and is very soft, especially if the meat has first been brined. The fried celery is quite unusual but the warmth from the caraway and the crunch really work.

SERVES 4

600g pork cheeks, trimmed
  of fat
1 tablespoon vegetable oil
1 onion, finely chopped
4 garlic cloves, finely
  chopped
1 tablespoon salt
a sprig of thyme
3 bay leaves
200ml cider
500ml stock
4 tablespoons olive oil
4 teaspoons white
  wine vinegar
4 celery stalks, trimmed
a pinch of caraway seeds
sea salt

for the basil oil

30g basil leaves
1 tablespoon grated
  Parmesan cheese
300ml olive oil
a pinch of salt

First brine the cheeks for 4 hours in a 10 per cent brine – that is, 10 per cent salt-to-water ratio. Place the cheeks in a large pot or basin and pour in enough water (measured) to cover it. Add 100g salt for each litre of water and leave uncovered in the fridge for 4 hours.

Preheat the oven to 150°C Fan (170°C/Gas Mark 3).

Rinse the brine off the cheeks and pat them dry. Heat the vegetable oil in a medium-sized, ovenproof pot on moderate heat until hot but not quite smoking. Now add the cheeks to sear them until all sides are golden brown (about 4 minutes). Remove the cheeks and set aside.

In the same pan, in the remaining oil, fry the onion and garlic, adding the salt, thyme and bay leaves. Once the vegetables are softened, add the cider and reduce until fairly dry – mostly absorbed into the vegetables. Next, add the stock and return the cheeks to the pot. Stir and allow to come up to the boil. Put the lid on the pot and place in the oven to cook for 2 hours.

Now make the meat vinaigrette. Remove the cheeks and strain the sauce into another pot; discard the solids. Put the pot on the stove top over a high heat and reduce the sauce down to about 100ml. Pour the sauce into a bowl, add 3 tablespoons of the olive oil and the vinegar and stir to mix. Set the meat vinaigrette aside and put the cheeks in the (turned-off) oven to keep warm.

Next make the basil oil. Using a stick blender, blend the basil leaves, Parmesan and olive oil together until thoroughly combined. Add a pinch of salt and stir, then pass the oil through a sieve to give it a smooth consistency. Refrigerate until ready to serve.

Cut the celery stalks into 2cm pieces. Add the remaining tablespoon of olive oil to a frying pan. Over a high heat fry the celery, adding a pinch of sea salt and the caraway seeds, for 1 minute.

Serve the cheeks on top of the celery and drizzle over a generous amount of the meat vinaigrette and the basil oil. Add a final sprinkle of sea salt and serve.

lamb sweetbreads, peas and pickled cucumber

'Sweetbreads' is one of the world's great misnomers. They sound so delicious and they are, but perhaps not in the almost sugary dessert way that many might expect. They are, of course, the glands (thymus or pancreas) of an animal (typically a lamb or calf), and are savoury sweet and quite delicious.

Lamb sweetbreads go very well with cucumber and peas. And adding the kaffir lime and the sweet, sticky Indonesian kecap manis really sets off the vibrancy of the fresh peas.

SERVES 4

500g lamb sweetbreads
1 cucumber
Jack's house pickle (see
    page 257)
200g peas, defrosted if frozen
1 kaffir lime leaf
50g butter
1 teaspoon kecap manis
    (sweet soy sauce)
1 tablespoon sunflower oil
4 sprigs of thyme
sea salt

to garnish

2 tablespoons crispy shallots
    (see page 253)

Rinse the sweetbreads under cold water for 5 minutes. Place in a saucepan and cover with water. Bring the water up to a simmer (80°C), then remove from the heat.

Strain the sweetbreads and leave to cool. Once they are cool enough to handle, peel off the outer membrane and discard. Set the sweetbreads aside.

Halve the cucumber lengthways and scoop out the seeds with a spoon. Cut into half moons about 2cm thick and place in a pot with the pickling liquid and warm up over a high heat until just before the boiling point, then remove from the heat and leave to cool in the pot.

Place the peas in a saucepan with 50ml water, the kaffir lime leaf, 25g butter, the kecap manis and a pinch of salt. Cook until the peas are soft but still have a little bite.

Add the sunflower oil to a frying pan and cook over a medium heat until hot. Now add the sweetbreads and fry for 2 minutes. Add the remaining butter and the thyme and turn the sweetbreads over. Allow the butter to foam and cook the sweetbreads for another 2 minutes, using a spoon to baste them with the butter while cooking. Remove from the heat.

Spoon some peas on to each serving plate; top with the sweetbreads and pea shoots, and serve the pickled cucumber in a separate dish alongside.

rack of lamb with pinot noir sauce

This dish was inspired by a visit I made to a vineyard in South Western Australia where they used little sheep to trim the vines. In the spirit of 'what grows together goes together', I came up with this dish. It's like a classic stew, just with the ingredients cooked separately and combined at the last minute. I like my lamb rack to be pink. Here I have used a traditional method of cooking it, but for the same result you could instead put the racks in a cooler oven (60°C Fan) and leave them for four hours, then sear them in foaming butter to colour and caramelise.

SERVES 4

8-bone rack of lamb
50ml vegetable oil
150g carrots, roughly
    chopped
150g onions, roughly
    chopped
150g celery, roughly chopped
1 leek, roughly chopped
4 garlic cloves, chopped
1 bouquet garni
500ml pinot noir
500ml chicken stock (see
    page 259)
a handful of dried porcini
    mushrooms
2 teaspoons dark soy sauce
1 teaspoon Marmite
    or Vegemite
star anise-glazed carrots (see
    page 242)
salt and pepper

for the kale
1 shallot, sliced
vegetable oil
200g kale, roughly chopped
salt and pepper

Preheat the oven to 200°C Fan (220°C/Gas Mark 7) and place a roasting tin inside to heat.

First, make the gravy. Pour 3 tablespoons vegetable oil into a large pot, then add the chopped carrots and onion and season them with salt. Add the celery, leeks and garlic. Stir through, then add the bouquet garni.

Pour 500ml wine into the gravy and let it reduce over a medium heat. Once it has reduced to a few tablespoons turn the heat down to low. When the liquid has almost entirely been absorbed, add the chicken stock, then the porcini mushrooms, the soy sauce and the Marmite or Vegemite. Leave to simmer over a low heat until it's reduced and thickened. Remove from the heat and pass the gravy through a sieve, squeezing out any excess liquid from the vegetables (discard these).

Meanwhile, cut the rack of lamb into 2 equal pieces. Sear in a hot pan in the remaining 2 tablespoons vegetable oil for 5 minutes, then transfer to the heated roasting tin. Roast for 15–20 minutes, or until the internal temperature reaches 56°C (for medium-rare) on a meat thermometer. Once it's cooked, remove the lamb from the oven, season with salt and pepper and rest for 15 minutes.

Now prepare the shallot for the kale. Place the sliced shallot in a small heatproof cup and just cover with the vegetable oil. Microwave for 30 seconds to make a confit.

Place the kale in a deep, wide saucepan with a splash of water. Season with salt and pepper, cover with a lid and let it steam over a medium-low heat for 2 minutes. Remove any leftover water from the kale and add the confit shallots and toss through.

Slice the lamb between the ribs and arrange a few slices on each plate, along with the kale and the carrots and a good drizzle of the red wine sauce.

lamb shoulder with white miso cream and chicory

If not on the barbecue a lamb shoulder should be cooked low and slow in an oven. For all those would-be barbecuers out there, for a dish like this one, you should first cook the meat in a normal oven for four-fifths of the time stated in the recipe, then just sear the hell out of it on the barbecue for the last one-fifth to give it a really good charred flavour.

Braised chicory is one of the first things I was taught to cook in a traditional French way by section chef Ben Towill at The Seafood Restaurant. He had just come from Raymond Blanc's Le Manoir Aux Quat Saisons and was a real influence on me at the start of my career. When it comes to chicory, you cut and trim them and then fry them in a little oil and butter to colour and then finally braise them in stock; this prevents the leaves from oxidising and changes the bitter note to a sweet one.

The white miso cream in this recipe is addictive and simple; it complements the lamb and chicory perfectly. And the lovely pink pickled onions make the dish look so appealing.

SERVES 4

2kg lamb shoulder
6 garlic cloves, peeled but
   left whole
6 sprigs of thyme, cut in half
6 anchovies, cut in half
1 tablespoon olive oil
4 chicory
1 tablespoon vegetable oil
60g butter
500ml chicken stock
   (see page 259)
juice of 1 lemon
1 tablespoon salt
sea salt

for the white miso cream
300ml double cream
300ml chicken stock
   (see page 259)
1 teaspoon white miso paste
50g butter

to serve
1 red onion pickled (see Jack's
   house pickle, page 257)

Preheat the oven to 200°C Fan (220°C/Gas Mark 7).

Make about 10 cuts in the lamb shoulder and push the garlic, thyme and anchovies into the cuts. Season with 20g salt, rub with the olive oil and roast in the oven for 30 minutes. Lower the temperature to 140°C Fan (160°C/Gas Mark 3) and cook for another 2½ hours.

Cut the chicory in half lengthways and remove the core (which is bitter). Brown them, cut side down, in a pot with the vegetable oil for 5 minutes. Add the butter and cook for 1 more minute. Now add the stock, lemon juice and salt, and turn the chicory halves over. Put the lid on and braise over a low heat until soft (20 minutes).

Now make the miso cream. Pour the double cream and stock into a pot; add the miso paste and whisk together. Cook over a medium-high heat, whisking occasionally. Keep on the heat until reduced by half, then remove from the heat and whisk in the butter. Pour into a serving dish.

Serve the lamb shoulder on the bone and carve at the table. Place the chicory alongside each serving, topped with slices of pickled red onion and pass round the dish of miso cream.

spring lamb casserole with new potatoes

It may seem unusual to have a casserole in spring, but this one fits the bill perfectly as it is light and full of the joys of the season. I like to make this when spring hasn't quite sprung to its full glory but just when the asparagus and peas and baby carrots are coming on to the market.

I suggest that this should really be made the night before the clocks go forward to welcome in the longer afternoons!

SERVES 4

1kg boned lamb shoulder, cut
    into 5cm cubes
20ml sunflower oil
1 carrot, chopped
2 onions, chopped
5 garlic cloves, chopped
2 bay leaves
800ml chicken stock (see
    page 259) or water
100ml dry white wine
1 tablespoon tomato purée
50g flour
50g butter
a sprig of thyme
10 small carrots, peeled with
    tops removed
50g fresh or frozen peas
50g French beans, topped
    and tailed and left whole
200g new potatoes, scrubbed
50g asparagus tips
salt and pepper

to garnish
a little chopped parsley
    and mint

First, working in batches, brown the meat in the sunflower oil in a large pot; season lightly with pepper. Transfer the browned meat to a plate or dish, then fry the chopped carrots, onions, garlic and bay leaves in the remaining oil until brown.

Meanwhile heat the chicken stock or water in a saucepan to simmering point.

Deglaze the first pan with the wine and allow the liquid to reduce until almost dry. Add the tomato purée and cook for 2 minutes. Then add the flour and butter and stir over a low heat to make a roux. Cook this for a further minute, then slowly add the hot stock, stirring to incorporate. Add a little salt and the thyme. Return the meat to the casserole, put on the lid and cook over a medium heat until the lamb is tender (about 1½ hours).

Towards the end of the cooking time cook all the spring vegetables in salted water. Just before serving, add them to the casserole and warm through. Check the seasoning and adjust if necessary. Serve the casserole with a sprinkling of chopped parsley and mint.

lamb breast, salsa verde and new potatoes

Breast is a very underused cut of lamb. It is quite fatty and works very well with long cooking. The best method is to tie it and roast it as a rolled joint; in this way it keeps its shape and is easier to serve.

I absolutely love salsa verde with lamb; anchovies and garlic are great friends of this meat. The following recipe is perfect for a spring roast, when the new season potatoes are available. Some say that Jersey new potatoes are the best; but I disagree, the best new potatoes come from Cornwall!

SERVES 4

1.6kg lamb breast, trimmed
of excess fat
a bunch of thyme, leaves
stripped from the stalks
1 tablespoon vegetable oil
salt

for the salsa verde

20g flat-leaf parsley, roughly
chopped
10g tarragon, roughly
chopped
40g capers, chopped
6 anchovy fillets, chopped
2 cloves of garlic, finely
chopped
120ml extra-virgin olive oil
1 tablespoon English mustard
1 tablespoon plus 1 teaspoon
lemon juice
$\frac{1}{2}$ teaspoon salt

to serve

300g new potatoes
a handful of mint leaves
2 tablespoons butter
sea salt

Preheat the oven to 180°C Fan (200°C/Gas Mark 6).

Score the meat into a criss-cross pattern. Rub with thyme leaves and salt. Cut the lamb in half crossways, and roll each half and tie with string to secure the shape.

Add the vegetable oil to a frying pan and sear each side of the meat in this, over a high heat until golden brown. Place the joints in a roasting tin and cook in the oven for 1½ hours.

Meanwhile prepare the salsa verde: put the parsley, tarragon, capers, anchovies and garlic into a bowl, then stir in the olive oil, mustard and lemon juice. Season and refrigerate until needed.

In the last 15 minutes of cooking the belly, prepare the potatoes. Wash and place in a pot with mint leaves and a pinch of sea salt, cover with cold water and bring to the boil. Reduce to a simmer and continue cooking for 15–20 minutes or until tender.

Remove the lamb from the oven and allow to rest for 15 minutes, covered with foil.

Drain the potatoes and transfer to a serving bowl. Add the butter and a pinch of salt (if needed) and mix to cover each potato, being careful not to break them.

Remove the string and slice the lamb into thick rounds; serve with the potatoes alongside. Top the meat with the salsa verde.

lamb liver, chestnut mushrooms and marmite butter

I used to hate almost all forms of offal. Once, when I was six or seven years old, I was given some so called 'sausages'. It turned out that they weren't sausages but rather lambs' testicles. It took me many years to get over my offal prejudice; however, once you have tasted perfectly cooked liver, you'll love it and realise how wonderful it can be.

Liver is great for Sunday brunch to start yourself off on activities such as walking the dog or, especially in autumn, foraging for mushrooms. We used to look for mushrooms a lot as children. We rarely found many, but one time I did find a massive horse mushroom; with hindsight it was probably about 30cm in diameter, but to me as a small boy it seemed about three times that size.

This recipe includes making a Marmite butter which can be made in advance and stored in the freezer.

SERVES 4

100g unsalted butter,
  softened
1 teaspoon Marmite
a dash of Worcestershire
  sauce
400g lamb liver
1 tablespoon vegetable oil
200g chestnut mushrooms
1 shallot, chopped
1 garlic clove, chopped
a sprig of thyme
1 teaspoon English mustard
juice of ½ lemon
sea salt

to serve

4 slices of toasted
  sourdough bread
a handful of chopped flat-
  leaf parsley, to garnish

In a bowl combine the butter, Marmite, a pinch of salt and Worcestershire sauce; mix well.

Cut the liver into 4 pieces and season them with salt. Heat the vegetable oil in a frying pan over medium-high heat. Once it is smoking-hot, cook the liver for 30 seconds on each side. Then add half the Marmite butter to the pan and turn the liver every 30 seconds for another 2 minutes. Baste the liver with the butter for the last 30 seconds of cooking. You want it to be pink.

Remove the lamb liver and let it rest in a warm place while you prepare the mushrooms.

Remove excess fat from the pan; add the mushrooms and stir them in the remaining fat. Add the chopped shallot and garlic, the thyme, the mustard and the other half of the Marmite butter, and cook, stirring, for 2 minutes. Squeeze over the lemon juice; stir through.

Cut the liver into thick slices. Place some mushrooms on each plate and top with a few slices of liver and a slice of toasted sourdough. Finish with a sprinkling of parsley.

dirty goat chop with sumac, pomegranate and feta cheese

When I was helping to research my father's India cookbook we found that many traditional Indian dishes use goat. Quite often lamb or mutton is substituted over here as goat is not always readily available in the UK. I always thought this was a bit of a shame as it's a really delicious and flavoursome meat. As chance would have it an old contact from my Sydney days quite recently founded an award-winning company called Cabrito that now supplies our restaurants with wonderful goat meat. You can make the same recipe with lamb or pork chops if you can't get hold of goat. We call the result 'dirty' because we cook the meat directly on charcoal. To achieve the same effect in your kitchen, just make sure to give the meat lots of time in the pan so that it's well coloured.

SERVES 4

zest of 2 lemons
25g salt
8 (2.5cm-thick) rib or loin
   goat (or pork or lamb)
   chops, about 100g each
a little olive oil

for the vinaigrette

2 tablespoons extra-virgin
   olive oil
2 teaspoons pomegranate
   molasses
½ teaspoon salt
1 teaspoon lemon juice

for the feta cream

50g finely crumbled feta
   cheese
100ml double cream
100ml milk
½ teaspoon salt
1 tablespoon lemon juice

to garnish

a handful of pomegranate
   seeds
a small bunch of mint leaves
a good pinch of sumac

Light 1kg of hardwood charcoal in the barbecue; it will be ready when grey ash forms. Meanwhile, mix the lemon zest and salt together in a bowl; set aside.

Make a vinaigrette with the oil, pomegranate molasses and lemon juice. Season with salt to taste and set aside.

Whisk the cream until it's semi-thick. Stir in the feta, milk, salt and lemon juice, and pass the cream through a sieve. Refrigerate until a few minutes before serving; it will need to soften a little so you can spoon it easily.

When the charcoal is ready, cook the chops directly on the coals without oil, 2 minutes on each side for pink. Once coloured, remove the chops and brush with the oil. Season with the lemon and salt mixture.

To serve, place a large dessertspoonful of the cream – or a quenelle if you're feeling fancy – on the side of each serving plate and lay 2 chops in the middle, one on top of the other. Drizzle the vinaigrette around the edge of the plate, leaving a little extra in a small pouring jug to add more if desired. Finish with sumac, pomegranate seeds and mint.

beef short ribs

Short ribs used to be a quid each but they have become so popular now that the price has risen. Fillet it seems has had its day and the time of the short rib has arrived. How the culinary world has come full circle!

The meat is cooked on the bone, low and slow, and served with curry leaves and a rich bordelaise sauce. The pickled onions cut through the fattiness of the meat and the crispy shallots add a great crunch.

A luxurious and special dish to share with food-loving friends partnered with some fine bottles of wine from the cellar – or the cupboard under the stairs.

SERVES 4

4 beef short ribs
50ml sunflower oil
2 teaspoons sea salt
500ml beef stock (see page 259) or water
200g pickled red onions (see Jack's house pickle, page 257)

for the bordelaise sauce
50g butter
2 shallots, finely chopped
a sprig of thyme
200ml red wine
500ml beef stock (see page 259)
1 teaspoon Marmite
1 tablespoon soy sauce
1 teaspoon salt

to serve
roasted new potatoes with seaweed salt and vinegar (see page 251)
a handful of crispy shallots (see page 253)
a few curry leaves

Pre-heat the oven to 150°C Fan (170°C/Gas Mark 3).

Pan-fry the ribs in the sunflower oil until coloured all over. Season them with the sea salt. Place the ribs on a baking try and add the water/stock before covering the tray with foil. Roast them until tender (4 hours), checking and adding more liquid if necessary.

To make the sauce, begin by melting the butter in a pan. Add the shallots and thyme and cook until the shallots soften, about 10 minutes. Next add the red wine and simmer until it has evaporated. Add the stock and reduce by around three-quarters, until you have about 150ml left. Add the Marmite, soy and salt to season.

Serve the ribs with the bordelaise sauce, pickled onions and new potatoes, and garnish with crisply shallots and curry leaves.

my roast topside of beef

This is my way of cooking a topside. It is placed in the oven at 9am and then left until we are ready for our roast at around 3pm. The topside, though quite cheap, can be a slightly tough cut for roasting, so I strongly recommend that you speak to your friendly local butcher and ask him to source one that has been dry-aged for a minimum of 21 days, preferably 30.

Set your oven to the temperature that you want the meat to end up (see the guidelines below). First sear it, paying attention to getting those lovely caramel reactions in the meat, then season it and put it in the oven. This method also tenderises the meat: as the meat temperature reaches 30°C, enzymes in it start to age the muscle. You can never overcook the meat if you set your oven to the temperature you want it to achieve.

SERVES 4

1.5kg topside of beef
1 tablespoon sea salt
1 tablespoon vegetable oil

for the gravy
2 shallots, finely chopped
2 garlic cloves, finely
   chopped
a sprig of thyme
1 tablespoon vegetable oil
1 teaspoon salt
375ml red wine
1 litre beef stock (see
   page 259)
1 teaspoon Marmite
2 teaspoons soy sauce
1 tablespoon rice
   wine vinegar
50g unsalted butter, cold

to serve
roast potatoes (see page 248)
steamed greens with confit
   shallots (see instructions
   for kale, page 176)

Preheat the oven to 55°C and season the beef all over with the salt. If you prefer your beef medium, set it to 60°C and so on. If your oven doesn't go this low, roast the beef at 220°C Fan (240°C/Gas Mark 9) for 30 minutes, then drop to 180°C Fan (200°C/Gas Mark 6), and roast until a meat probe reads 55°C, which should take about 1½ hours.

Heat the oil in a frying pan and sear the beef on each side until golden brown (about 2 minutes each side including the ends). Deglaze the pan with 2 tablespoons water; reserve these pan juices for making the gravy later.

Put the beef into a roasting tin and cook in the oven for a minimum of 4 hours until the internal temperature reaches the oven temperature you set.

Meanwhile roast the potatoes (see page 248). Set aside and keep warm.

When the meat is nearly finished, prepare the greens as described for the kale on page 176.

Now make the gravy. Soften the shallots, garlic and thyme in vegetable oil in a saucepan over a medium heat and season with the salt. Add the red wine and reduce until evaporated. Add the beef stock and deglazed pan juices and reduce by half. Add the Marmite, soy sauce and vinegar and reduce by another one-quarter. Whisk in the cold butter to finish.

After removing the beef from the oven, leave it to rest for 15 minutes.

Slice the beef (thick or thin, as you like) and serve with the greens, roast potatoes and gravy.

sirloin on the bone with baked potato and tomato salad

Once while I was doing a cooking demo, someone asked me what I would choose for my last meal. I replied that it would be sirloin on the bone – but cooked over the fire at La Tupina in Bordeaux, where even the chips are cooked on coals.

This recipe is a mix from all over the place – just how I like it! The way the steak is cooked is an amalgam of classic French cooking (the foaming butter and thyme) and the modern methods of chefs such as Heston Blumenthal (flipping it every 20 seconds to keep the meat evenly cooked). The baked potato's liberal dusting of sea salt on the top comes courtesy of my grandmother, Dorrie. The salad was the first thing I made at university, when I had discovered the pleasure of choosing ingredients, chopping, dressing and seasoning correctly.

I always give my baked potatoes a quick blast in the microwave first. It reminds me of a quote by the wonderful and sorely missed comedian Mitch Hedberg: 'It takes forever to cook a baked potato. Sometimes I'll put one in the oven even if I don't want it, because by the time it's done, who knows?!'

I just love this meal!!

SERVES 4

4 baking potatoes
150g butter, softened
4 (280g) sirloin steaks on
    the bone
30ml sunflower oil
4 sprigs of thyme
sea salt and pepper

for the salad

300g cherry or vine-ripened
    tomatoes
2 tablespoons aged balsamic
    vinegar
1 (125g) ball of mozzarella,
    sliced about 5mm thick
1 shallot, thinly sliced
a handful of fresh basil
olive oil

Preheat the oven to 200°C Fan (220°C/Gas Mark 7).

Put the potatoes into the microwave for 10 minutes on full power. Place them on a baking tray and cover them with a little butter, using your hands or a spoon; add lots of sea salt and pepper. Bake for 30–45 minutes until golden brown. (If you don't have a microwave, cover them – raw – with the butter and seasonings and bake for 2 hours.)

Meanwhile make the salad. Slice the tomatoes and cover in salt and balsamic vinegar. Allow to macerate until ready to serve. Combine the mozzarella with the shallot and the basil. Toss the salad all together and drizzle with a little olive oil.

Cook the steaks 2 at a time in a solid-based frying pan. First season them generously with salt only. Heat a little sunflower oil in the pan over a high heat until the oil starts to smoke. Place the steaks in the pan and cook, turning every 20 seconds; this ensures an even heat distribution. After 90 seconds add 2 sprigs of thyme and 50g butter, and continue to turn the steaks every 20 seconds. Reduce the heat to medium when the butter starts to foam, and start to baste while turning. Cook for another 90 seconds (for medium-rare), continuing to baste and turn. Remove from the heat. Transfer the steaks to a warm plate or wooden board and leave them to rest while you cook the other 2 steaks.

Serve the steaks with a baked potato and salad alongside. Make sure you put lots of butter in each potato!!!

osso bucco

The first time I went to Italy my initial evening meal was an osso bucco. I was hooked! This is a really great way of making a meal for a special occasion, such as New Year's Eve, when you're cooking for lots of people. It's made of beef shin, which is a cheap cut, but the long cooking time it requires is transformative. Serve it with saffron barley risotto (see page 128), and see how happy you make your friends and family! This recipe is easily scaled up if you want to serve a crowd.

SERVES 6

50g plain flour
a large pinch of sea salt
4 tablespoons olive oil
1.8kg beef shin, bone in, cut
   in thick rounds
4 celery stalks, diced
3 carrots, diced
1 onion, diced
3 bay leaves
a bunch of thyme
1 star anise
250ml dry white wine
2 (400g) cans of tomatoes
500ml beef stock (see
   page 259)
1 tablespoon plain flour
salt

to serve
saffron barley risotto (see
   page 128)
zest of 2 lemons
a handful of chopped parsley

Combine the flour and sea salt on a plate, then dredge the shin rounds in the flour.

Heat 2 tablespoons of the olive oil in a deep pot over a medium-high heat. Once hot, add the shins and turn until all sides are browned, then transfer to a plate. Turn the heat down to medium and add 1 tablespoon olive oil and the celery, carrots, onion, bay leaves, thyme and star anise; season with salt. Cook for 20 minutes, stirring occasionally. Add the wine and allow to reduce completely then add the tomatoes and stock. Add the beef shin back to the pan, bring to the boil, then reduce the heat to very low, cover and cook for 2 hours, stirring occasionally.

Put 1 tablespoon flour in a glass and pour 2 tablespoons olive oil over it, mixing with a fork to make a smooth paste. Uncover the pot and add the oil paste, stirring it through. Cook for 15 minutes, uncovered, until thickened.

Serve on top of the risotto, sprinkled with the lemon zest and parsley.
Buon appetito!

beef cheeks with horseradish mash

Beef cheeks are an inexpensive and very good cut of meat but if you can't get hold of them you can use brisket instead. I would always recommend asking your local butcher for odd and interesting cuts of meat – they are normally more than happy to sell you the offcuts that no one else uses. It's also well worth trying to find cheeks that have been dry-aged, so ask for a 30-day-aged beef cheek; it will be softer and have a lot more flavour.

The gravy here is finished with ketchup butter – the butter and ketchup help to thicken the sauce and add some sweetness and richness.

SERVES 4

800g beef cheeks, trimmed
1 tablespoon vegetable oil
1 tablespoon olive oil
1 onion, diced
2 carrots, diced
bouquet garni of bay leaves
    and thyme
3 garlic cloves, sliced
375ml red wine
100ml marsala
1 litre beef stock (see
    page 259)
2 tablespoons ketchup butter
    (see page 253)
sea salt

to serve
mashed potatoes (see
    page 249)
1 teaspoon horseradish sauce

Preheat the oven to 180°C Fan (200°C/Gas Mark 6).

Season and sear the beef cheeks in the vegetable oil in a deep, ovenproof pot with a lid until golden brown, then remove the cheeks and set aside.

Add the olive oil to the pot, along with the onions, carrots and bouquet garni. Cook on a medium-low heat for 10 minutes. Add the garlic and cook for another 5 minutes.

Add the red wine and marsala and allow to reduce until evaporated. Add the beef stock and cheeks. Put the lid on the pot and cook in the oven for 2 hours.

Transfer the cheeks to a serving dish and cover to keep warm.

Pass the sauce through a fine sieve into a saucepan. Using the back of a spoon, press the vegetables in the sieve to release all the flavour and juices. Skim off the fat from the sauce and place the pan over a medium-high heat to reduce it by one-half to the consistency of gravy. Once reduced, add the ketchup butter and stir it through until well blended.

Prepare the mashed potatoes, then stir the horseradish sauce into them.

Spoon the potatoes into each bowl and top with the beef cheeks, then pour the gravy over them.

bone marrow with toasted rice and sweet and sour sauce

Bone marrow is another of those cuts of meat that are shockingly under-used. Many people find it quite unappealing; however, I love to set myself the challenge of turning something resistible into something truly wonderful. Often the easiest way to achieve this is to turn to Thailand for inspiration.

This is a simple sweet-and-sour dish with a bit of a larp feel (see page 64), thanks to the toasted rice. The smooth bone marrow needs the crunch provided by the apple, and the tamarind glaze is perfect whilst they roast in the oven. Trust me – even my mum, who hates bone marrow, went for these!

SERVES 2 (OR 4 AS A STARTER)

25g long-grain rice
1.4kg bone marrow, split in 2,
    each piece portioned into
    4 pieces about 10cm long
1 tablespoon sunflower oil
2 teaspoons sea salt

for the sweet-and-sour sauce

75g tamarind paste
1 tablespoon sugar
juice of 1 lime
1 bird's-eye chilli
2 tablespoons fish sauce
1 banana shallot, cut into
    very small cubes
½ carrot, cut into very
    small cubes

to garnish

1 apple, peeled, cored and
    cut into batons
a few Thai basil leaves

In a saucepan, heat the tamarind paste, sugar, lime juice, chilli and fish sauce until the sugar has dissolved. Then remove from the heat and add the chopped shallots and carrots. Set aside.

Preheat the oven to 200°C Fan (220°C/Gas Mark 7).

Put the raw rice in a dry pan, over a medium-high heat, and toss until slightly puffed up. Using a pestle and mortar, slightly break up the puffed rice and stir in a touch of salt.

Season and oil the bone marrow pieces, transfer them to a baking tray and place in the oven for 10 minutes. Take the tray out of the oven and lightly dress the marrow with the sweet-and-sour sauce, reserving a tablespoonful for drizzling later. Put the tray back in the oven for another 2 minutes.

Place 2 pieces of the bone marrow on each plate and lay the apple batons across them. Drizzle them with the remaining sauce and garnish with the puffed rice and Thai basil leaves.

pigeon breasts and vodka-macerated berries

I invented this dish many years ago for the final of a chefs' competition at Earls Court in London. I was completely out of my depth and I'm pretty sure that all of my dishes contained some fundamental cooking error! What's more, when I was plating up, Jocky and Stefan, two friends from The Fat Duck, in Bray, turned up and put me off, and flustered I left off one of the key elements of the dish. The legendary two-star Michelin chef Sat Bains was judging, and he let me know unequivocally that I had made a huge blunder… But despite this initial setback I really think this dish now works wonderfully well. The maceration of fat berries in vodka and fructose makes the berries taste riper. The combination of earthy beetroot and piquant pickled shallots really sets off the pigeon breast. On top of all this is the fact that the dish looks so evocatively autumnal. It may have been a flop in the competition but it's well worth trying, using all the ingredients!

SERVES 4

½ pomegranate
60g blackberries
60g blueberries
1 tablespoon vodka
1 teaspoon fructose sugar
1 shallot
2 tablespoons Jack's house
    pickle (see page 257)
250ml beetroot juice
½ teaspoon sugar
1 tablespoon cider vinegar
3 tablespoons rapeseed oil
a pinch of sea salt
4 pigeon breasts
1 tablespoon vegetable oil
1 tablespoon butter
a sprig of thyme

Place the pomegranate half, cut side down, on a chopping board and strike the husk with a wooden spoon or the handle of a knife to release the seeds. Place them in a bowl (discard the husk).

Halve the blackberries and place in a bowl with the pomegranate seeds and the blueberries. Pour over the vodka and fructose sugar and stir to combine. Leave for 1 hour to macerate.

Slice the shallot crossways. Warm up the pickling liquid in a small pan and immerse the shallot slices in it. Remove from the heat and leave to cool.

Put the beetroot juice in a saucepan placed over a high heat and reduce to a little over 2 tablespoons, so it is thickened to a syrupy consistency. Add the ½ teaspoon sugar and stir to dissolve. Allow to cool.

Put the beetroot juice, cider vinegar, rapeseed oil and sea salt in a bowl. Stir to combine.

Season the pigeon breasts with sea salt and add the vegetable oil to a frying pan placed over a high heat. Once it is hot, add the pigeon breasts. Fry them for 1 minute, turning them every 10 seconds; then reduce the heat to medium and add the butter and thyme. Baste the pigeon breasts with the foaming butter for 2 minutes. Remove from the heat and allow to rest for 3 minutes.

Slice each pigeon breast on an angle into 4 or 5 slices and place on serving plates; top with the pickled shallots and place the berries and pomegranate seeds alongside. Finally dress each plate with beetroot vinaigrette.

sweets &
cheeses

plum tart with brown anglaise butter

With a filling of just mascarpone and honey this is
a wonderfully easy plum tart to make and bake.
Usually I prefer my plums simply drizzled with honey
and baked, but this is a great alternative and can be
made well in advance. The browned butter crème
anglaise uses a trick I learned while in Scandinavia.
To make browned butter you normally cook the butter
until the solids start to brown and smell nutty. Here,
you add protein to the solids in the form of milk powder
and then cook it to the usual level. When infused into
a crème anglaise it acts as a wonderful counterpoint to
the acidity in the plums. You could also churn this into
an ice cream base to make browned butter ice cream.

SERVES 8

170g flour, sifted, plus extra
  for dusting
a pinch of salt
100g cold unsalted butter,
  cubed
50g caster sugar, plus a little
  extra for caramelising
1 egg yolk
50ml double cream
5 large plums, 4 cut in half
  lengthways, 1 crossways,
  stones removed (or more
  plums if small)
500g mascarpone cheese
6 tablespoons clear honey

for the crème anglaise

250ml double cream
75g caster sugar
1 vanilla pod, cut in half
  lengthways, seeds removed
  and reserved
6 egg yolks
50g unsalted butter
50g skimmed milk powder

First make the pastry. Combine the flour, salt and butter in an electric mixer, using the dough hook, starting at a slow speed, then increasing the speed as the ingredients come together. Add the sugar and continue mixing until the pastry resembles fine breadcrumbs. Add the egg yolk and cream to the flour mix until it comes together to form a dough. (Alternatively use a wooden spoon, then your hands to bring it together.)

Have ready a loose-bottomed 20cm tart tin, the bottom lined with a circle of baking parchment. On a floured surface, roll the dough out to a 25cm diameter circle. Push it well into the bottom of the tin and trim off the excess around the rim. Cover the tin with cling film and refrigerate for at least 30 minutes.

For the crème anglaise, pour the double cream into a saucepan and add ½ teaspoon of the sugar and the seeds from the vanilla pod. Bring it up to a simmer over a medium heat. Then add the pod itself for extra flavour and let the mixture simmer for about 5 minutes. Remove from the heat and set aside.

In a mixing bowl, whisk together the egg yolks and the rest of the sugar until they just come together. Slowly pour the cream into the egg and sugar mix, whisking until combined, then transfer into the saucepan. Place over a medium heat and cook, stirring constantly, until the mixture thickens enough to coat the back of a spoon. Remove the crème anglaise from the heat and pass it through a sieve to catch the vanilla pod halves (discard these). Set aside.

Now make the browned butter. Place the butter in a pot over a low heat until it starts to brown, bubble and foam (about 1 minute). Add the skimmed milk powder, stirring quickly to combine. As soon as the mixture begins to resemble breadcrumbs remove it from the heat. Add it to the crème anglaise, and use a stick blender to pulse together. Pass the mixture through a sieve to remove any lumps and place it in the fridge.

Preheat the oven to 180°C Fan (200°C/Gas Mark 6). Remove the pastry from the fridge. Place another circle of baking parchment on the base. Fill with baking beans and blind-bake the pastry for 10 minutes. Remove the beans and the paper circle and bake for 3–5 minutes. Remove from the oven and lower the temperature to 160°C Fan (180°C/Gas Mark 4).

Place the plum halves together, cut side up, on a baking tray. Sprinkle a little sugar over them and caramelise this with a blowtorch.

For the filling, soften the mascarpone with the honey in a saucepan over a low heat. Pour this into the pastry case, then lay the plums on top, cut side up, with the round half in the centre (eat the other!) Bake for 30 minutes or until the pastry edges start to golden. Allow to cool, then remove it from the tin and serve with the crème anglaise on the side.

elderflower and strawberry fool with cornish fairings

A fool is a very old English dessert, first recorded in the 1590s. Traditionally, it is made with gooseberries, but other fruits can be used. You can layer your chosen fruit with crème anglaise, but I prefer to use whipped cream instead for a much easier and lighter dessert.

Elderflower is one of those reminders of summer often come across growing wild whilst walking in the countryside. But be careful if you plan to forage as elderflower has a similarity to the potentially deadly hemlock. So if you are looking for wild elderflower, it might well be safer and easier to buy from a shop!

Cornish fairings are very easy to make and keep well.

SERVES 6

for the fairings (makes 28)
225g plain flour
½ teaspoon salt
1 teaspoon baking powder
1 teaspoon bicarbonate
  of soda
2 teaspoons mixed spice
1 tablespoon powdered
  ginger
1 teaspoon cinnamon
125g unsalted butter
125g caster sugar
120g golden syrup

for the fool
400g strawberries, stems
  removed
55g caster sugar
1 tablespoon lemon juice
a pinch of cracked pepper
5 mint leaves, chopped
300ml double cream
75g clotted cream
220ml elderflower cordial

First make the fairings. Preheat the oven to 170°C Fan (190°C/Gas Mark 5).

Sift all the dry ingredients, except the sugar, into a bowl. Rub in the butter with your hands until the mixture looks like breadcrumbs. Stir in the sugar.

Warm up the golden syrup in a saucepan over a low heat and pour it into the dry mixture. Combine, again using your hands, to form a smooth dough.

Roll out the dough to a thickness of about 7–8mm. Use a small 6cm cookie cutter to cut out the fairings. Re-roll to cut more. You should have about 28. Place the fairings on a floured baking tray and bake in the oven until golden brown (about 8–10 minutes). Leave them for 10 minutes to harden up before transferring to a cooling rack.

Now make the fool. Mash half the strawberries with a fork, along with the sugar and lemon juice to make a sort of marinade or purée.

Slice the rest of the strawberries and add them to the strawberry marinade. Add the cracked pepper and mint leaves. Leave for 15 minutes.

Put the double cream, clotted cream and elderflower cordial into a bowl and whip into stiff peaks.

Have ready 6 glasses. Place a layer of strawberries in the bottom of a glass and then a layer of cream. Repeat until you reach the top of the glass, finishing with a layer of cream. Crumble some Cornish fairings over the top. Enjoy!

strawberries with clotted cream, miso and nori

This wonderful recipe shakes up the favourite traditional British dessert of strawberries and clotted cream. Modern cooks use a lot of savoury elements in desserts nowadays, all kicked off by the popularity of the now ubiquitous salted caramel. Here I simply incorporate some miso into the cream. The wonderfully rich clotted cream from Rodda's in Cornwall is the best available and well worth seeking out. I once went on a factory tour of Rodda's and, as we got to the ovens in which they bake the cream to get the crispy top, I asked the guide at what temperature the ovens were set. He immediately exclaimed that this was a secret recipe and that he could not possibly divulge the information. Then I spied a recipe sheet behind his head and said innocently, 'So it's not baked for [x] minutes at [x] degrees and then for [x] minutes at [x].' He couldn't believe how I knew this secret formula and looked mortified so I put him out of his misery and confessed shortly afterwards – I wonder if that sign is still there!

I have used nori sheets, readily available in supermarkets, to add even more savouriness to the dish. These are the edible seaweed sheets used for sushi. It's best to use sheets from a new, unopened packet, as you'll find them easier to break up.

SERVES 4

1 sheet nori seaweed
4 tablespoons icing sugar
10g sweet white miso
200g clotted cream
800g strawberries, halved

Rub the nori sheet to break it up and form a fine powder. Mix this with the icing sugar and reserve.

Combine the miso and the clotted cream in a bowl.

Dust the strawberries with the nori sugar and serve the cream alongside.

crème brûlée with papaya

This recipe comes from our head pastry chef, Stuart Pate. Crème brûlée has always been a favourite of mine –even more so the Spanish crema Catalana version, which comes with a lovely citrus hit. Stuart's interpretation features lime zest and adds papaya. It's a simple and delicious triumph!

If you are serious about making crème brûlée part of your repertoire, do make the effort to get a MAPP gas gun; they are used by roofers, and you can easily find them online. They burn at a higher temperature than ordinary blowtorches and make the topping very easy to caramelise.

SERVES 4

6 medium egg yolks
35g sugar
2 tablespoons caster sugar
300ml double cream

to serve
1 papaya
zest (finely grated) and juice
  of 1 lime
60g sugar

Preheat the oven to 100°C Fan (120°C/Gas Mark ½).

Mix the egg, sugar and cream together, using an electric mixer or by hand. Pour into 4 brûlée dishes or ramekins, place in a deep baking tray. Fill with enough water to reach halfway up the sides of the ramekins and cook in the oven for 20–25 minutes (keep checking every 5 minutes) until set. They should be firm but with a slight wobble when moved.

Peel and deseed the papaya and cut the flesh into 1cm cubes. Place in a bowl and mix in the lime zest (reserving a little to serve) and juice and the sugar.

When ready to serve, sprinkle the caster sugar over the brûlées and caramelise with a blowtorch.

When the caramel has set, spoon some of the papaya cubes on top. Sprinkle over the remaining lime zest and serve.

blood orange cheesecake

It is always hard to find things to make in the winter that are seasonal. I remember one winter being with a great friend, Ollie Hutson, who runs the kitchen gardens for The Pig hotel chain, and when walking through one of their gorgeous conservatories in the walled garden came across a tree bearing a solitary blood orange. Ollie said that during winter it is hard to find citrus fruits, but as long as that blood orange tree is growing there, he has a supply, albeit limited, of blood oranges. So this cheesecake is a nod to Ollie. It's pretty simple but has a bit of gelatine in the base to stabilise it (you can substitute agar agar for the gelatin if you are making the cake for vegetarians).

You can buy lemon curd if time is an issue but it is always worthwhile to try and make your own.

SERVES 12

for the base
100g digestive biscuits
50g butter, melted

for the filling
250g cream cheese
75g caster sugar
375g double cream
½ vanilla pod, split, with
    seeds scraped out and
    reserved
1 gelatine leaf

for the jelly
500ml blood orange juice
2 gelatine leaves

for the orange crumb
1 orange, peeled
50g digestive biscuits
30g white chocolate

for the lemon curd
50g caster sugar
zest of 2 lemons
1 egg
50ml lemon juice
50g butter, cut into cubes

First make the base of the cheesecake. Place the digestive biscuits in a food processor and blitz until you have fine crumbs. Transfer to a mixing bowl, add the melted butter, and mix thoroughly. Spread the mixture out over the bottom of a rectangular pan about 20 x 30cm in size and set aside.

For the filling, whisk together the cream cheese and sugar until well combined. Slowly add the cream, whisking until the mixture forms soft peaks. Remove a little of the mixture and melt it down in a pan along with the vanilla seeds and pod. Soak the gelatine in cold water for 10 minutes, then squeeze out the water and add the gelatine to the pan. Remove the vanilla pod, then pour this mixture back into the cream cheese mixture and fold it in. Pour the filling on to the base and smooth the top. Chill it in the fridge until it is set, about 2 hours.

Now make the jelly. In a saucepan over a medium heat bring the blood orange juice to a simmer, then lower the heat and let it simmer until it has reduced to a purée (about 30 minutes; you need about 250ml). Bring the purée to the boil and immediately remove it from the heat. Soak the gelatine as described for the filling and stir it into the purée. Allow it to cool slightly, then pour it over the cheesecake. Chill it in the fridge until set (overnight would be best).

For the orange crumb, first peel the orange and reserve the segments. Place the peel on a baking tray in an oven set as low as it can go for 20–30 minutes until completely dry. Blitz it in a blender, along with the digestive biscuits and white chocolate. Set aside.

For the lemon curd, combine the sugar, lemon zest, egg and lemon juice in a saucepan and cook over a medium heat to 85°C. Allow it to cool to room temperature (about 20 minutes), then add the cubed butter and blitz it with a hand blender.

To serve, cut the cheesecake into 12 portions and decorate them with orange segments. Sprinkle some of the orange crumb alongside, then add the lemon curd, using a piping bag to make teardrop shapes or dot it on with a spoon.

peanut butter and chocolate cheesecake with salted caramel and popcorn

Sometimes in life you have to make a quick decision; this dessert is a good case in point. We were prepping to photograph the desserts for this book in London and I had slightly miscalculated the number of desserts – we were one short. I knew that the ingredients I had in mind would combine beautifully, so I opened the fridge at the restaurant and extracted a slice of cheesecake, poured a little caramel into a tub and legged it to the shoot, leaving a small note saying, 'Took one slice of cheesecake, won't be able to replace, thanks.'

If you're making this dessert from scratch, you'll need to start it the day before serving.

MAKES 1 CHEESECAKE

for the base

150g digestive biscuits, crushed
3 teaspoons cocoa powder
100g unsalted butter, melted

for the filling

60g smooth peanut butter
150g caster sugar
500g mascarpone
25ml double cream
1 teaspoon vanilla essence

for the topping

100ml double cream
100g dark chocolate drops

for the salted caramel sauce

100g granulated sugar
45g unsalted butter, at room temperature
60ml double cream
½ teaspoon salt or more to taste

to serve

purchased ready-made popcorn: 10g per person
a little icing sugar

Mix all the base ingredients together and push into a loose-bottomed, 23cm flan tin. Chill in the fridge for 2 hours.

Beat the peanut butter and sugar together in a food mixer until light in colour. Add the mascarpone, cream and vanilla and mix slowly until just incorporated (over-mixing will cause it to split). Smooth it over the cheesecake base. Chill for 2 hours.

Heat the cream and the chocolate drops together in a saucepan over a low heat, stirring until combined. Leave the mixture to cool for 10 minutes, then pour it evenly over the cheesecake. Chill for 12 hours.

Now make the salted caramel sauce. First heat the sugar in a saucepan over a medium heat, stirring it continuously with a spatula or wooden spoon.

As soon as the sugar has dissolved and is a dark brown, thick liquid, add the butter straight away. The caramel will start to bubble. Keep stirring until all the butter has melted and been incorporated into the caramel.

Slowly pour in the double cream, still stirring. Keep on heat for another minute; the mixture will bubble and rise in the pan. Remove from the heat and stir in the salt, then allow to cool. You can always add more salt, depending on your taste. The caramel can be stored in the fridge overnight along with the cheesecake. It makes about a cupful and will keep for 1 week. Any left over would make a great topping for ice cream.

Shortly before serving, place the popcorn in a large bowl and stir in a little salt and icing sugar to taste. Remove the cheesecake from the fridge and let it sit for a few minutes to make it easier to cut. Place a slice on each plate. Warm up a little salted caramel – either in a small pot on the hob or in a small bowl in the microwave for 30 seconds–1 minute until it is loose enough to drizzle over the cheesecake but not so hot that it would melt the chocolate layer. Add some salty, sweet popcorn to each plate and dig in!

JACK STEIN'S *World on a Plate*

individual pavlovas with redcurrants and sea buckthorn

This dish reminds me so much of my early visits to Australia, where the pavlova seems to be a national obsession. We first had it with passion fruit somewhere in Sydney and since then it has become a staple in our restaurants back in the UK. So how to 'Britify' a dish like this? The closest thing we get to passion fruit here is sea buckthorn, a small berry that grows in the car parks around the Cornish coast. You can make your own juice, but I don't recommend it if you like a clean kitchen – just buy some online. Or honour the pavlova's origins with passion fruit juice.

SERVES 4

3 egg whites
a pinch of salt
175g caster sugar
1 teaspoon cornflour
½ teaspoon white
    wine vinegar
300ml double cream

to decorate
4 sprigs of redcurrants
60ml sea buckthorn juice
    or passion fruit juice

Preheat the oven to 140°C Fan (160°C/Gas Mark 3).

Line a baking tray with baking parchment.

In a large mixing bowl, or electric stand mixer fitted with the whisk attachment, whisk the egg whites, along with the salt, until they form stiff peaks. Gradually whisk in all the caster sugar. The meringue mixture should be stiff and shiny. Now whisk in the cornflour and, finally, the vinegar.

Place 4 large spoonfuls of the mixture on the baking tray and spread each one out with the back of the spoon so they are roughly 10cm in diameter. Bake for 45 minutes until they have just turned cream in colour and are soft and spongy in the centre. Turn off the oven and leave the tray of meringues inside, with the door half open, until they are cool.

Now whip the cream to a until it's thick. Spoon some into the centre of each pavlova and spread it out a little – not too much, as the topping will push it out more. Add the whole redcurrants; you can pick them off the stem if you like, but I quite like the look of the stem and redcurrants lying across the top, as shown. Pour over the sea buckthorn, or passion fruit, juice. And enjoy.

pineapple tarte tatin with coconut sorbet

A tarte Tatin is always a wonderful thing. It is one of those desserts that just works in any situation. Flexible and adaptable, tarte Tatin can be made with very many different fruits. I love cooked pineapple and I think it works beautifully here.

SERVES 6

250g puff pastry
75g butter, softened
175g caster sugar
1 medium-sized pineapple

to serve
vanilla ice cream or
    crème fraîche

Roll out the pastry on a lightly floured surface and cut out a 26cm disc, slightly larger than the top of a 20cm tarte tatin dish or reliably non-stick cast-iron frying pan. Transfer to a baking sheet and chill for at least 20 minutes.

Meanwhile, spread the butter over the base of the tarte tatin dish or frying pan, and sprinkle over the sugar in a thick, even layer.

Cut the top and bottom off the pineapple, trim the skin off the side and slice into rounds, each about 5cm thick.

Tightly pack the pineapple slices into the tarte tatin dish or frying pan and place over a medium heat. Cook for 20–25 minutes, gently shaking the pan now and then, until the butter and sugar have mixed with the pineapple juices to produce a rich sauce and the pineapple is just tender. At first the caramel will be pale and there might be some liquid from the juices of the pineapple, but as you keep on cooking, the juices will evaporate and the butter and sugar will become darker and thicker. Just take care that the butter and sugar do not burn. When the pineapple has been caramelised, remove the pan from the heat.

Pre-heat the oven to 170°C Fan (190°C/Gas Mark 5).

Gently place the pastry on top of the pineapple slices and tuck the edges down inside the pan. Prick the pastry 5 or 6 times with the tip of a small, sharp knife, transfer to the oven and bake for 25 minutes, until the pastry is puffed up, crisp and golden.

Remove the tart from the oven and leave it to rest for 5 minutes. Run a knife round the edge of the tart and invert it onto a round, flat serving plate. Serve warm, cut into wedges, with crème fraîche or vanilla ice cream.

panna cotta with berries and coconut crumb

This delicious panna cotta just screams 'autumn' to me. Usually we simply add a few plums to our panna cotta, however my partner, Lucy, came up with this new version of the Piedmontese classic, adding berries and a coconut crumb. This not only makes the dish look delicious but also contributes to it tasting delicious.

SERVES 4

for the panna cotta
2½ gelatine leaves
425g double cream
25g caster sugar
215ml milk
1 whole vanilla pod, split
   lengthways and seeds
   scraped out and reserved

for the coconut crumb
30g plain flour
30g butter, cold, cut
   into cubes
30g caster sugar
30g coconut flakes/chips

for the berries
100g blackberries
100g blueberries
1 teaspoon caster sugar

to decorate
a few mint leaves

First make the panna cotta. Soften the gelatine in cold water for a few minutes, then wring out the water. Place the cream, sugar, milk, vanilla pod and seeds in a saucepan over a low heat and bring to 38°C. Remove from the heat and stir in the gelatine. Allow to cool.

When the mixture thickens, take out the vanilla pod. Stir to distribute the vanilla seeds evenly, then pour the mixture into ramekins and chill in the fridge overnight.

For the coconut crumb, place the flour and butter in a bowl and rub them together with your fingers until the mixture resembles breadcrumbs. Add the sugar and coconut and mix through. Spread on a tray lined with baking parchment and bake until golden (about 10–15 minutes). Remove from the oven and leave to cool. Once cool, crumble up with your hands and set aside.

Cut the blackberries and blueberries in half and combine in a bowl. Sprinkle the sugar over them and mix together.

To turn out the panna cottas, dip the bottom of the ramekin into a pan of hot water for a few seconds. Turn the ramekin over on to a serving plate, pat the base and slowly lift. If the panna cotta doesn't come out, try patting it again or put it back into the water for a few more seconds.

Add some berries and coconut crumb to each plate and garnish with a few mint leaves.

elvis sandwich

This may or may not be an authentic Elvis sandwich, so I'll avoid the issue and just proclaim it as my very own version of an Elvis sandwich (famously and notoriously a combination of sweet and savoury fillings). We used to enjoy eating them occasionally when I was a sous chef at our café in Padstow. Back then the idea of combining bacon and honey was very alien to me. Then about five years ago the world went bonkers for meat and sweet, and suddenly bacon jams were everywhere. This is a treat of a sandwich. Please don't count the calories … and let me know if you manage to eat more than one!!

SERVES 4

16 rashers of unsmoked
   bacon
100g butter
8 slices of ordinary
   white bread
50g peanut butter
2 bananas, sliced diagonally
20g honey

Fry the bacon in 1 tablespoon butter in a pan until crispy; place the rashers on kitchen paper to drain, leaving the fat and juices in the pan.

Add the remaining butter to the same pan and fry the slices of bread until golden brown and crispy. Transfer to a plate and set aside.

Warm the peanut butter in the same pan, then set aside. Using a new frying pan, warm the banana slices in any leftover butter from frying the bread, or add another tablespoon if required.

Assemble the fillings on one slice of bread and drizzle the honey over them. Place the other slice on top, put the sandwich back in the second pan and turn it, just to warm up the outside briefly.

Place each sandwich on a serving plate and cut it in half.

chocolate pavé

This dish was created by a chef called Bruce who once worked for us. It's easy to make and who doesn't like the blissful combination of chocolate, coffee, peanuts and ice cream? To make the crystallised peanuts successfully you'll need to use electronic scales to measure the ingredients precisely. You can make the peanuts in advance; they will keep in an airtight container for a month or so.

SERVES 8

130g unsalted butter,
    softened
125g caster sugar
1 shot espresso
50ml honey
80g bitter cocoa powder
a small pinch of salt
120g egg yolks
225g double cream
70g dark chocolate

**for the crystallised
peanuts**
62g roasted peanuts
4g caster sugar
a small pinch of salt
33g caster sugar
½ teaspoon golden syrup

to serve
vanilla ice cream
crushed digestive biscuits

First make the crystallised peanuts. Toss the peanuts, sugar and salt together in a bowl.

Put the last caster sugar and golden syrup in a saucepan with 23g water, stir to dissolve the sugar, then bring to the boil over a high heat until the syrup measures 140°C on a sugar thermometer.

Add the peanut mixture to the sugar syrup and stir continuously over a low heat until the sugar crystallises and turns white (about 5 minutes). Tip the nuts on to a sheet of silicone release paper. Using a spoon, separate the nuts while warm. Store them in an airtight jar until required.

Line a shallow rectangular dish with a sheet of cling film large enough to come over the sides. Set aside.

Next, beat the butter and sugar in a food mixer fitted with the paddle attachment over a high speed until light and fluffy. Beat in the espresso and honey. Now reduce the speed and add the cocoa powder and salt.

Add the egg yolks and beat until they are well incorporated and the mixture is smooth. Transfer to a large bowl and set aside.

Using a hand mixer or a whisk, whip the cream until stiff, and set aside.

Melt the chocolate gently in a microwave (at 30-second intervals, stirring after each, so as not to burn); alternatively melt it in a bain-marie. Quickly fold the chocolate into the cream, then carefully fold this into the butter and sugar mixture until evenly combined; do not overwork.

Spoon the dessert into the lined dish and put it in the refrigerator to set for a few hours.

When ready to serve, bring it out of the fridge and leave it for a few minutes, then pull up the cling film edges to release the pavé. Turn it on to a large plate and cut it into thick slices. Serve the portions with the peanuts sprinkled on top and vanilla ice cream on a bed of crushed digestives alongside.

choco bars

I like choco bars, any kind of choco bar. If you don't like glacé cherries or want to experiment you can include any other extras you like in the bars – chopped nuts perhaps or even Malteasers. Or you can simply keep them plain using only raisins; they will still be delicious! Enjoy them just as they are, with a mug of coffee, or dress them up for dessert with additional cherries and other red fruits and maybe some crumbled biscuits on top.

MAKES 16 (10 X 2.5CM) BARS

225g digestive biscuits, plus
    more to serve (optional)
110g salted butter
2 tablespoons sugar
2 tablespoons golden syrup
4 teaspoons cocoa powder
a handful of raisins
a handful of halved glacé
    cherries, plus more
    (optional) to serve
150g milk chocolate
150g dark chocolate

Roughly break up the digestive biscuits and place them in a plastic bag. Then, using your hands (or lightly with a rolling pin), crush the biscuits even more, to a crumb consistency, but not too fine. It's okay if there are still a few bigger pieces.

Next, melt the butter and sugar in a saucepan over a low heat. As the butter begins to soften and melt, stir in the golden syrup. Now add the cocoa and mix it all together. Turn off the heat once everything is combined. Add the crushed biscuits, raisins and cherries to the chocolate mix and stir through until everything is evenly coated.

Pour the mixture into a 20cm-square or comparable rectangular baking dish or tin and spread it around with a spoon. Press down with your hands to cover the bottom of the dish and push the mix into the corners so it's level and compact.

Fill a saucepan about one-quarter full with water and set it over a medium-low heat. Place a heatproof bowl over the pan, making sure the bottom doesn't touch the water. Break up the milk and dark chocolate, add them to the bowl and stir until melted together.

Pour the melted chocolate over the biscuit base. Pick up the dish and angle it each way to make sure the melted chocolate flows into all the corners and covers the biscuit base.

Place the tray in the fridge for 2–3 hours.

When ready to eat, remove the dish from the fridge and cut the cake into long bars or squares. Serve them either plain or dressed up with more glacé fruits and a dusting of crushed digestive biscuits.

milk chocolate mousse with macadamia nuts and glazed bananas

Chocolate mousses are my kind of dessert – partly because they can be made in advance and won't split, flop, fall over, scramble or submit to any other affliction. They also allow me to demonstrate my one outstanding skill in the pastry area: the one-handed quenelle, or rocher (as they are called in France).

Heat a large spoon by sticking it in hot water and then use the side of the ice cream or mousse container to roll it up to form a perfect egg shape.

You can either have a go at learning to make a rocher yourself or simply serve the mousse as a scoop – it will taste just as good!

You will need to start preparing this dessert a day before serving.

SERVES 4

285g milk chocolate
635ml double cream
100g macadamia nuts
1 teaspoon butter
2 bananas (½ per person)
1 tablespoon caster sugar
zest of 1 orange

For the mousse, first heat the milk chocolate over a water bath until melted. Heat 150ml double cream in another saucepan over a medium-low heat, stirring occasionally, until just before the boiling point. Remove from the heat, stir into the melted chocolate, then transfer to a mixing bowl (preferably stainless steel). Stir in the remaining double cream and place in a rectangular storage container. Leave in the fridge overnight to set.

Lightly crush the macadamia nuts. Melt the butter in a frying pan and add the nuts. Sauté them over a medium-high heat for 30 seconds, spooning the butter over, until they are well coated and golden brown. Remove from the pan and drain on kitchen paper.

Slice the bananas and spread them out on a shallow baking tray. Lightly sprinkle them with the caster sugar and caramelise with a blowtorch. Allow the slices to cool, then carefully lift them up with a spatula and spread them out in a crescent shape on individual plates.

Place a quenelle of mousse next to the glazed banana slices, or, if you don't fancy tackling the quenelle, spoon the mousse on to the side of the plate. Spoon some macadamia nuts alongside the mousse and sprinkle orange zest over each plate. Enjoy straight away!

asparagus with bacon and miss muffet cheese

The arrival of fresh asparagus heralds the start of spring. As we come out of the lean winter period we start to get a slow but steady increase into our kitchens of wonderful new season vegetables. The key to cooking asparagus is to poach it in oil. If you boil it in water you may notice that the water starts to taste of asparagus. If, instead, you poach it in oil the flavour doesn't leak out.

I pair this asparagus with Miss Muffet, which is a hard-ish cheese from Bude, in Cornwall, along with some crispy bacon lardons.

While I was in Paris I was taught to boil the bacon briefly before frying as it removes some of the water and fat. By doing this, and then patting the lardons completely dry, it enables the bacon to crisp up far better when it's pan-fried.

SERVES 4

2 litres olive oil, plus a little
    for pan-frying
800g asparagus, woody lower
    end trimmed off
200g streaky bacon
100g Miss Muffet or other
    semi-hard cheese
½ tablespoon sea salt

Put the olive oil into a deep pan and warm to 60°C; do not allow it to boil. Add the trimmed asparagus spears and cook for another 5 minutes – very, very gently poaching them. Remove the asparagus from the oil and drain on kitchen paper.

Cut the bacon crossways into lardons, and place in a pan full of cold water. Bring to the boil, then strain the bacon. Transfer to a plate and pat dry with kitchen paper. Pan-fry the lardons in a little oil until crispy; reserve.

Using a peeler or cheese slicer, slice the cheese into thin strips.

Serve the asparagus while still hot with the crispy bacon and the cheese on top. Season with sea salt.

miss muffet cheese with truffle

For me there is nothing better than a cheese course. This recipe is inspired by a truly great man, Paul Cunningham. I ate something approximating to it in his old restaurant The Paul, in Copenhagen's Tivoli Gardens. This dish is like a sourdough cracker pizza, but I use a the Cornish hard cheese Miss Muffet. It's as close as we get in England to a Parmesan cheese.

SERVES 4

1 sourdough loaf
extra-virgin olive oil,
    for drizzling
100g rocket
200g Miss Muffet cheese
    or Parmesan
a Wiltshire black truffle, or
    20g minced truffle from
    a jar, or a good drizzle of
    truffle oil
a handful of pickled red
    onions (see Jack's house
    pickle, page 257)
sea salt and pepper

Preheat the oven to 180°C Fan (200°C/Gas Mark 6).

Slice the sourdough very thinly. Rub the slices with a little olive oil to help them brown and bake in the oven for 15–20 minutes until golden brown and crisp.

Place the slices on a huge serving platter. Dress the rocket with a little olive oil and sprinkle the salt and pepper on top. Arrange the rocket on top of the bread. Shave the cheese generously all over the rocket, and then shave the black truffle on top (or spoon the minced truffle/drizzle the oil on top). How much you give your guests can depend on how much you like them – at least that seems to be the custom in France and Italy!!!

Finish with some pickled red onion and serve.

baked camembert

I absolutely love baked cheese in any guise. This is a great winter starter for a supper party as it requires the minimum of effort. Melted cheese with thyme is just a magical thing to eat. This is a little like an easy-to-make fondue. The toasted sourdough bread can be broken up and dipped into the cheese, along with the pieces of potato.

SERVES 2

100ml olive oil
1 teaspoon thyme leaves
8 slices of sourdough bread
2 Camembert in wooden
    boxes (or ceramic dishes)
1 teaspoon sea salt

to serve

100g boiled new potatoes
    (skin on), cut into wedges
100g pickled red onions
    (see Jack's house pickle,
    page 257)

Pour the olive oil into a small pot, add the thyme leaves, and warm gently, just to a simmer, to infuse the oil with the thyme. Remove from the heat.

Brush the slices of sourdough with some of the warm thyme oil and toast them on both sides under a grill.

Preheat the oven to 200°C Fan (220°C/Gas Mark 7).

Remove the packaging from the cheeses and place them back into the wooden boxes. Score the skin of the cheeses and drizzle with a little of the thyme-infused olive oil. Place them on a baking tray and bake in the oven for 10 minutes. Alternatively you can microwave them for 2 minutes. Finish with a sprinkling of sea salt.

Serve with wedges of new potatoes, the sourdough and pickled red onions.

british cheese tartiflette

Tartiflette is a classic dish from the Alps, a behemoth of melted cheese, bacon, pickles, tomatoes and potatoes. When I was working as a chef in the Swiss Alps, my one day off a week would involve lots of wine and a little skiing on the way to Cabane du Mont-Fort, in Verbier, where we would stop for this dish. We called it a holiday day because we acted like we were regular skiers on holiday, but we would be asleep by 7pm to get enough sleep ready for another 6 days straight of work!

This is a one-pan meal but contains a staggering number of calories, so if you are not skiing maybe have it only once in a while!

SERVES 6

1kg potatoes, peeled and
   cut into quarters
200g smoked bacon, cut
   into lardons
2 red onions, peeled and
   thinly sliced
3 garlic cloves, sliced
1 teaspoon thyme leaves
200ml dry white wine
6 vine-ripened tomatoes,
   quartered
500g mature Cheddar, sliced
   2cm thick
salt and pepper

to serve
a handful of cornichons
a handful of pickled
   silverskin onions

Preheat the oven to 180°C Fan (200°C/Gas Mark 6).

Cook the potatoes in well-salted water and keep warm until needed.

Meanwhile, place the lardons in a saucepan in cold water and bring to the boil, immediately strain through a sieve and allow to dry.

In a large frying pan or casserole dish that can go in the oven, dry fry the lardons until crisp. Remove the lardons and use the remaining fat to fry the onions, garlic and thyme over a medium heat until softened (add a little sunflower oil if necessary). Add half the wine and reduce until it has disappeared.

Add the lardons back into the pan and now add a layer of potatoes and tomatoes to the pan and season with salt and pepper. Arrange the slices of Cheddar on top and pour in the rest of the wine. Place the frying pan or casserole in the oven and cook until the cheese is browned and melted (about 30 minutes).

Finish the tartiflette with the cornichons and silverskin onions.

sides &
stocks

star anise–glazed carrots

These carrots are so special they can form the centrepiece of a vegetarian feast. The key is to allow the water to evaporate until it's pretty much gone and the butter, sugar and salt have made a glaze.

Star anise provides a wonderful background note to these carrots. Try it with heritage carrots for an even better flavour. As a lot of the flavour of root vegetables is in the skin you don't need to peel new-season carrots, just rub them under running water.

SERVES 4

16 whole baby carrots,
    topped and tailed
1 teaspoon salt
20g sugar
50g unsalted butter
1 star anise

Place the carrots in a saucepan large enough to hold all of them flat. Just barely cover with water, then add the salt, sugar, butter and star anise. Bring to the boil, uncovered, then reduce to a low simmer. The carrots will be finished and ready to eat when all the liquid – or nearly all – has evaporated (about 10 minutes). Test by inserting a knife through the thickest part of a carrot. If it slides through fairly easily, remove the carrots and plate them. The butter, sugar and salt will have formed a glaze. (Discard the star anise.) Any remaining liquid (if of a syrupy consistency) can be drizzled over the carrots.

tenderstem broccoli with crispy shallots and parmesan

SERVES 4

400g tenderstem broccoli
1 tablespoon olive oil
1 teaspoon sea salt
10g crispy shallots (see
    page 253)
25g Parmesan cheese, shaved

Place the broccoli in a saucepan with 25ml water, cover and steam for 1 minute. Then heat the oil in a frying pan until hot, fry the broccoli for 3 minutes and season with the salt. Sprinkle the crispy shallots and Parmesan on top.

griddled hispi cabbage with mirin and soy

SERVES 4

1 hispi cabbage
120ml vegetable oil
50ml mirin
25ml soy sauce
1 teaspoon sugar
½ tablespoon sea salt

Cut the cabbage into quarters and brush the cut sides with a little of the vegetable oil.

Make a dressing with the mirin, soy and the remaining vegetable oil and dissolve the sugar in it.

Place a griddle pan or frying pan over a medium-high heat. When it is hot, fry each cut side of the cabbage until well coloured but not cooked through. You want them to be still crispy and have some bite. While they are cooking, spoon some of the dressing on to them.

Arrange the cooked cabbage on a serving platter. Drizzle the rest of the dressing over them and season with the salt.

roast potatoes

Before I put potatoes in the oven for roasting I give them a good 15–20 minutes in rapidly boiling water, so that the outsides are nice and fluffy ready to soak up the oil while roasting. I add the skins loose to the water because, as with all root vegetables, a lot of the flavour is to be found in the skins. I roast the skins along with the potatoes – crispy potato skins are a chef's treat while cooking.

SERVES 4

800g Maris Piper potatoes
25g sea salt
50ml sunflower oil
25ml goose fat (optional)
   at room temperature

Peel the potatoes (reserving the peelings) and cut them into chunks (cut in half if small, into quarters if large). Pour 2 litres of water into a saucepan, add 20g salt, and bring to the boil. Add the potatoes and the peelings. Cook for 15–20 minutes until the potatoes are fluffy on the outside but still holding their shape. Strain off the water very gently, then allow the potatoes and peelings to cool to room temperature.

Meanwhile preheat the oven to 200°C Fan (220°C/Gas Mark 7). When this temperature has been reached, pour the sunflower oil into a roasting tin and place it in the oven for 15 minutes.

Add the potatoes, cut sides down, to the hot oil and cover with the oil. (They will sizzle!) Add the skins at the same time. Season the potatoes with the remaining salt and roast for 60–90 minutes, turning them a few times, so that all sides are immersed in the oil for 30 minutes.

For better flavour, pour over the goose fat for the last 10 minutes. Drain the potatoes well on kitchen paper.

mashed potatoes

SERVES 4

800g Maris Piper potatoes
5 teaspoons salt
200ml double cream
200ml milk
50g butter

Peel the potatoes and cut them into chunks. Place them in 2 litres of water in a large pan, along with 4 teaspoons salt, and bring to a simmer. Cook until soft (about 25 minutes); don't let the water boil.

Meanwhile put the cream, milk, butter and the remaining teaspoon of salt in a pan and bring to just below a simmer over a low heat. Remove from the heat and cover to keep warm.

When the potatoes are cooked, drain them and push them through a ricer or mash with a potato masher. Then while all is still warm, fold half of the butter and cream mixture through the potatoes and whisk together, using either a hand whisk or a wooden spoon. Add the remaining butter and cream mixture (if needed), and whisk again to finish. Stir in a little more salt if needed.

roasted new potatoes with seaweed salt and vinegar

SERVES 4

20g salt
800g new potatoes, scrubbed
50ml vegetable oil or beef
   dripping
2 teaspoons Cornish
   seaweed salt
20ml malt vinegar

Preheat the oven to 200 °C Fan (220°C/Gas Mark 7). Place a roasting pan in the oven to heat.

Meanwhile, add 2 litres of water and the 20g salt to a large pan and bring to the boil. Add the potatoes and parboil for 10 minutes, then drain and allow to cool.

Remove the roasting pan from the oven, add the vegetable oil or dripping and return the pan to the oven.

Once the oil is hot, add the potatoes to the roasting pan and carefully turn them in the oil. Add the seaweed salt and cook for 20–30 minutes until the potatoes are well browned.

Take the potatoes out of the oven and drizzle with malt vinegar. The potatoes go perfectly with some white fish, such as cod.

miso mayonnaise

MAKES 600ML

2 egg yolks
1 tablespoon English
   mustard
1 teaspoon miso paste
1 teaspoon salt
500ml vegetable oil
1 tablespoon cider vinegar

Place a damp tea towel under a large mixing bowl and add the egg yolks.
Beat for a couple of minutes until creamy.

Add in the mustard, miso paste and salt and whisk again to combine. In a steady
stream, slowly pour the oil into the egg mix and whisk continuously until you
have a thick, glossy mayo. Add the cider vinegar and then taste, adjusting the
seasonings as necessary.

basa gede

This is a common Balinese spice paste, used in nasi goreng, soto ayam and babi galung.
You can buy it, but I think homemade is best.

MAKES ABOUT 200G

2 small shallots, roughly
   chopped
4 garlic cloves, roughly
   chopped
2 red chillies (medium heat)
5cm piece of ginger, peeled
   and roughly chopped
1 tablespoon roasted peanuts
1 tablespoon palm sugar
½ teaspoon shrimp paste
6 black peppercorns
1 teaspoon turmeric
1 teaspoon salt
a pinch of nutmeg
a pinch of sesame seeds
3 tablespoons vegetable oil
juice and zest of 1 lime

Blend all of the ingredients together in a food processor or mixer until you have
a smooth paste. Store in the fridge until required.

ketchup butter

This butter is perfect for finishing sauces. I also use it in gravies and with baked beans! Try it in anything; it adds the most wonderful balance to a dish because of the mix of sweetness, acidity and richness.

MAKES 250G

250g unsalted butter
25g ketchup
1 teaspoon Worcestershire
   sauce
1 tablespoon soy sauce
1 teaspoon Marmite

Soften the butter and mix with all the remaining ingredients. Roll into a log and wrap the butter in cling film. Store in the fridge or freezer until required.

crispy shallots

The feeling of a crunch between your teeth is so appealing; a roast potato or chip has some ethereal way of pleasing us. So to this end, it's important to have a few things you can go to in order to add texture to your dish. The following three recipes are a few things I have picked up from my travels.

You can buy crispy shallots, and in most instances I suggest you do! If you do want to give them a go, this is my recipe...

MAKES ABOUT 100G

1 teaspoon salt
100g shallots, peeled and
   sliced into rounds on a
   mandoline, or very finely
   with a knife
vegetable oil

Salt the shallots for 10 minutes, then wash and pat dry them with kitchen paper. In a pan, add enough oil to fill the pan to a depth of 5cm and heat it to 150°C.

Using a slotted spoon, slowly place the shallots into the oil. Keep them moving and fry for about 8 minutes until they go a light gold in colour, then remove. (Top tip: if you wait and take them out when they are the darker colour you think you want, they will keep cooking and burn.) Sprinkle with salt and leave to dry on kitchen paper in a warm, dry area. Like I said, it's easier to buy them.

crispy chicken skins

MAKES 250G

250g chicken skins
20g salt

Preheat the oven to 180°C Fan (200°C/Gas Mark 6).

Scrape the fat off the back of the chicken skins and place in a pan of boiling, salted water (around 2 litres). Reduce to a simmer and cook for 20 minutes.

Using a slotted spoon, lift the boiled skins out of the water, pat dry, place on a baking tray and lay another baking tray on top. Place the enclosed skins in the oven and bake for 20 minutes, then turn the skins over and bake, uncovered, for another 10 minutes. Remove from the oven and pat the skins dry with kitchen paper. Eat immediately or store in an airtight container for up to 1 week.

butter roasted nuts

MAKES 100G

1 tablespoon vegetable oil
100g nuts, such as cashews
25g butter
a pinch of salt

Warm the oil in a frying pan and add the nuts, tossing to coat them in the oil. As they start to sizzle add the butter and allow to foam. Keep moving the nuts around the pan, and if the butter starts to turn too brown, move the pan on and off the heat. Foam until the nuts turn golden then drain on a kitchen towel and season with a pinch of salt.

jack's house pickle

This is my house pickle recipe, and is a great one to have in your repertoire. With all pickles, the basics are vinegar, water, sugar and salt.

The best things to pickle are onions, shallots, cucumbers and beets but anything will pickle eventually. You can use these homemade pickles to add acidity to a dish where traditionally you might add lemon juice. Play around with the things in your pickle and make it your own.

This makes up a fairly large amount of pickling liquid, but it can be used again and again so it's worth making a full batch. Otherwise, feel free to just make half quantities.

MAKES ABOUT 1.1 LITRES

750ml rice wine vinegar
2 teaspoons salt
100g sugar
5 sprigs of thyme
2 star anise
a pinch of chilli flakes
5g dashi granules (1 sachet)

Pour the vinegar and 375ml water into a large pot. (As a general rule, work to a two-to-one vinegar to water ratio.)

Add the salt and the sugar, and then the thyme, star anise, chilli flakes and dashi granules.

Add whatever is being pickled at this point too. Bring to the boil and then remove from the heat, leaving it to steep for 10 minutes or leave to cool in the pickle liquid until needed.

You can reuse the same pickle juice over and over.

vegetable stock

MAKES 2.5 LITRES

2 fennel bulbs
2 onions
1 head of garlic, cut in
    half crossways
2 leeks
4 carrots
1½ tablespoons olive oil
2 star anise
2 bay leaves
2 sprigs of thyme
zest of 1 lemon

Finely chop all the vegetables and place them in a large pot, along with the olive oil, star anise, bay leaves and thyme. Soften them over a medium-low heat for 10–15 minutes; do not let them brown. Add 2.5 litres water and lemon zest. Leave to simmer, uncovered, for 2 hours. Strain off the liquid and refrigerate until needed.

fish stock

The smell of fish stock reminds me of being at home. Dad always has some sort of stock on the go. I like to use kombu to give it extra depth.

MAKES 2.5 LITRES

1 tablespoon vegetable oil
2 celery stalks, diced
2 leeks, diced
4 shallots, diced
a handful of button
    mushrooms
2 bay leaves
2 sprigs of thyme
1kg fish bones (preferably flat
    fish, gills removed), rinsed
    in cold water)
1 kombu sheet

Heat the vegetable oil in a big pan and add the vegetables, bay leaves and thyme; cook over a medium heat until soft but not coloured (5 minutes).

Add the fish bones, kombu and 2.5 litres water, and bring to a very gentle simmer; do not boil. Leave simmering for just 30 minutes. Remove from the heat and leave to rest for 1 hour, so that all the solids fall to the bottom. Then pour the stock through a sieve, leaving about 500ml and the solids in the pot; discard. Refrigerate the stock until needed.

chicken stock

To give this stock a slightly deeper flavour, use the bones from a roasted chicken.

MAKES 1.7 LITRES

bones from a 1.5kg uncooked
  chicken or 450g chicken
  wings or drumsticks
1 large carrot, chopped
2 celery stalks, sliced
1 kombu sheet
2 leeks, cleaned and sliced
1 onion, cut in half
  crossways, root to tip
2 bay leaves, fresh or dried
2 sprigs of thyme

Put all the ingredients into a large pan with 2.2 litres water and bring to the boil, skimming off any scum as it rises to the surface. Leave to simmer, uncovered, very gently for 2 hours – it is important not to let it boil, as this will force the fat from even the leanest chicken and make the stock cloudy. Strain the stock through a sieve and leave to simmer a little longer to concentrate the flavour if necessary (taste to check). If not using the stock immediately, leave to cool, then chill (it will keep in the fridge for 5 days) or freeze for later use.

beef stock

MAKES 2 LITRES

2kg beef bones
1 tablespoon salt
2 tablespoons vegetable oil
2 carrots, roughly chopped
2 onions, roughly chopped
1 head of celery, roughly
  chopped
2 bay leaves (fresh or dried)
2 sprigs of thyme
2 star anise
1 tablespoon tomato purée

Preheat the oven to 200°C Fan (220°C/Gas Mark 8).

Place the beef bones in a roasting pan and season them with the salt. Drizzle over 1 tablespoon oil and roast for 25–30 minutes. Set aside.

Meanwhile add all the vegetables and the bay, thyme and star anise to a pot, along with the remaining oil. Cook over a medium-high heat until the vegetables are slightly browned (about 10 minutes), then add the tomato purée and stir it through to coat the vegetables.

Add the bones and 4 litres water to the pot. Simmer for 6–8 hours, skimming occassionally. Strain off the liquid and refrigerate until needed.

index

acknowledgements

This book couldn't have happened without an army of people, and I would like to thank the following people in particular:

Marie O'Mara and Emily North at Absolute Press for chasing me and keeping me to deadlines; Jon Croft for having faith in me; and Bloomsbury for everything, including all their PR and marketing.

Borra and Jan at DML for their support throughout.

Casey Lazonick and Alva for all their help and constant visits to Waitrose.

The team at Rick Stein Barnes for allowing us to steal all their mis en place on the mornings of the photoshoot.

Paul Winch-Furness for being amazing in all he did, and for the between-shot entertainment.

Mum and dad for allowing me the freedom to do this.

Fred the dog, from Goa in 1992, for being my friend.

Colin and Stuart Morton for allowing us to use their lovely cottage for recipe testing.

All the people I have met in my 36 years that have shared recipes with me and inspired me.

And of course Lucy Musca for working on the recipes with me, assisting with the styling and food testing, and being generally wonderful.

about the author

Jack Stein, middle son of Rick Stein, is the Chef Director of the Stein Restaurant Group. He spent his early years travelling around the world with his family on trips to discover food in far-flung places whilst his father created and presented world famous TV cookery shows. A bug for food and travel was caught.

With food now firmly on his mind, Jack secured himself a stage at La Regolade in Paris which reignited a passion for travel and led him to take further stage work in leading restaurants all over the world, picking up culinary customs and traditions as he travelled. There then followed a period cooking at the legendary Tetsuya's in Sydney after which he began to explore the Far East and Japan, and a world gastronaut was born!

However, it wasn't long before Jack returned to his roots and embraced the simple ethos that his parents projected from their Cornish restaurant. Jack entered The Seafood Restaurant as sous chef before graduating to Chef Director. Working from the development kitchen Jack creates and perfects new recipes introducing his passion for the world's great cuisines into the menus of the restaurants using the best of British produce.

@JackStein

credits

Publisher Jon Croft
Commissioning Editor Meg Boas
Senior Editor Emily North
Art Director & Designer Marie O'Mara
Photographer Paul Winch-Furness
Photography Assistant Casey Lazonick
Food Styling Jack Stein and Lucy Musca
Prop Styling Matt Inwood
Recipe Editor Eleanor Van Zandt
Home Economists Adam Shepherd, Elizabeth Fox and Elaine Byfield
Proofreader Margaret Haynes
Indexer Zoe Ross

ABSOLUTE PRESS
Bloomsbury Publishing Plc
50 Bedford Square, London, WC1B 3DP, UK

BLOOMSBURY, ABSOLUTE PRESS and the Absolute Press logo
are trademarks of Bloomsbury Publishing Plc

First published in Great Britain 2018

A catalogue record for this book is available from the British Library.

Library of Congress Cataloguing-in-Publication data has been applied for.

ISBN   HB: 978-1-4729-4938-7
         ePub: 978-1-4729-4937-0
         ePDF: 978-1-4729-4936-3

2 4 6 8 10 9 7 5 3 1

Printed and bound in China by RR Donnelley Asia Printing Solutions Ltd.

Bloomsbury Publishing Plc makes every effort to ensure that the papers used
in the manufacture of our books are natural, recyclable products made from
wood grown in well-managed forests. Our manufacturing processes conform
to the environmental regulations of the country of origin.

To find out more about our authors and books visit www.bloomsbury.com
and sign up for our newsletters.